MANAGING YOUR PROFESSIONAL IDENTITY ONLINE

MANAGING YOUR PROFESSIONAL IDENTITY ONLINE

A Guide for Faculty, Staff, and Administrators

Kathryn E. Linder

Foreword by Laura Pasquini

STERLING, VIRGINIA

Published by Stylus Publishing, LLC.
22883 Quicksilver Drive
Sterling, Virginia 20166-2019

Library of Congress Cataloging-in-Publication Data
Names: Linder, Kathryn E., author.
Title: Managing your professional identity online : a guide for faculty, staff, and administrators / Kathryn E. Linder ; foreword by Laura Pasquini.
Description: First edition. | Sterling, Virginia : Stylus Publishing, LLC., [2018] | Includes bibliographical references and index.
Identifiers: LCCN 2018007114 (print) |
LCCN 2018022475 (ebook) |
ISBN 9781620366707 (Library networkable e-edition) |
ISBN 9781620366714 (Consumer e-edition) |
ISBN 9781620366684 (cloth : alk. paper) |
ISBN 9781620366691 (pbk. : alk. paper)
Subjects: LCSH: College teachers--Vocational guidance. |
College administrators--Vocational guidance. | Online identities. |
Self-presentation. | Personal information management. | Internet in higher education.
Classification: LCC LB1778 (ebook) |
LCC LB1778 .L56 2018 (print) |
DDC 378.1/2--dc23
LC record available at https://lccn.loc.gov/2018007114

13-digit ISBN: 978-1-62036-668-4 (cloth)
13-digit ISBN: 978-1-62036-669-1 (paperback)
13-digit ISBN: 978-1-62036-670-7 (library networkable e-edition)
13-digit ISBN: 978-1-62036-671-4 (consumer e-edition)

Printed in the United States of America

All first editions printed on acid-free paper
that meets the American National Standards Institute
Z39-48 Standard.

Bulk Purchases
Quantity discounts are available for use in workshops and for staff development.
Call 1-800-232-0223

First Edition, 2018

For Professor Linda Mizejewski,
who encouraged me as a young writer
and who has been cheering me on over many years

For Benjamin Winter,
who brings so much joy and humor to my life
and who never balks when I buy another domain name

And for Ralph Winter,
my model for calm under pressure
and because, finally, it's your turn

CONTENTS

TABLES, FIGURES, AND BOXES

Tables

Figures

Boxes

Have you thought much about your online self? Beyond developing a social media profile to network among scholars, higher education professionals and faculty are highlighting pedagogical practices, tracking research impact, supporting colleagues, and contributing to professional learning online. We are all public intellectuals now, in some shape or form, so it is critical to review the media for participation as digital scholars and networked practitioners.

Colleagues interested in creating an online presence should explore the wealth of social and digital resources available to connect to learning networks, exchange pedagogical ideas, and disseminate information. There are so many ways to craft an active, online profile to signal to peers and share within networked communities of interest.

Along with early career researchers and teaching faculty, applied practitioners are contributing to the growing network of knowledge in postsecondary education. A number of higher education staff and senior administrators use digital spaces to form personal learning networks and share evidence-based practices that deal with issues we face in higher learning, such as student retention, employment development, and financial costs of education. The motivation to join these "digital water coolers" is simple—social, digital platforms allow a direct connection to colleagues and resources in higher education. With the ease of these emergent technologies, we are now able to discover what colleagues beyond campus are working on, understand new perspectives for practice, and enhance our knowledge by broadening our online professional learning networks.

Hashtags have influenced how online communities use Twitter for learning and professional development. For example, student affairs practitioners host a weekly, moderated Twitter chat with the hashtag #sachat to discuss ways to support student services, offer career development advice, discuss program development, and provide personal/professional support for graduate students and practitioners (Guidry & Pasquini, 2016). The #phdchat hashtag offers doctoral researchers a space to distribute academic papers, promote events or publications, ask questions, offer productivity tips, share gratitude, and offer advice on teaching and learning (Veletsianos, 2016b). Additional higher education communities use Twitter to organize formal and informal discussions about academic advising (#acadv), learning and teaching (#lthechat), early career research (#ecrchat), enrollment management (#emchat), academic writing (#acwri), digital pedagogy (#digped), and more.

Beyond Twitter, a growing number of individuals and collective groups are gathering online, in synchronous and asynchronous ways, to learn and develop. Social and digital platforms often frequented by postsecondary peers include blogs, Facebook groups, presentation sharing sites, video channels, podcast series, image sharing (e.g., Flickr or Instagram), LinkedIn Groups, Slack back-channels, shared documents (e.g., Google docs or wikis), and reference sharing websites (e.g., Mendeley or Zotero). Increasingly, digital tools help higher education academics and professionals solicit information and seek out feedback or professional advice. There are academic-focused networking sites, such as Academia.edu and ResearchGate, that allow for preprint publication sharing, scholar identifications, comment/feedback requests, and tracking of research dissemination. On mainstream social networks, such as Facebook, Twitter, and YouTube, scholars and practitioners often display examples of instructional materials, student support resources, and applied evidence-based practices.

With the advent of social networks and online platforms also arrives the necessity to cultivate our individual digital identity. Your digital footprint is now your business card. What you leave behind on social networks and websites better showcases your experiences more so than a typical résumé or CV. Higher education scholars and practitioners are more conscientious of how to manage their online presence by aggregating research citations on ORCID, curating employment experiences on LinkedIn, and archiving research presentations or instructional materials on SlideShare. Spheres of influence and interest expand as social technologies and accessible web design allow staff and faculty the opportunity to develop a website hub for showcasing their talents, experiences, and skills. Unlike publications that remain dormant in an online database or strategic plans that get shared only within an institution, higher education professionals and academics now have the ability to become curators and broadcasters of knowledge. Open social outlets provide a wider reach for digital distribution, discussion, and debate among postsecondary educators. The barriers for reaching multiple audiences are often removed with these open, online, and interdisciplinary networks. Academics and professionals do not have to rely only on traditional methods for sharing knowledge and practice—that is, typically a conference meeting or scholarly publication. Digital and social spaces offer new ways to communicate, collaborate, create, and share knowledge across disciplines and functional areas in higher education.

As our networked, social spheres online mature, scholars and scholar-practitioners need to consider how to best operate in this evolving attention economy. Our institutions are not fully prepared to support higher education professionals and academics on these connected digital platforms. We need our organizations to offer learning development for crafting an online persona, strategies for effectively sharing knowledge, and increased guidance and support for being a networked practitioner and/or digital scholar. This education should also be paired with thoughtful conversations around both the benefits and challenges of sharing teaching, research, and service scholarship in open social spaces. This book encourages faculty and staff to consider how they want to "be" online, with practical questions, guiding strategies, and helpful links to digital resources. As members of the higher education community increasingly "live" online, personally and professionally, it will be increasingly critical to keep this conversation open to further understand how these virtual spaces influence and impact our practice.

Laura Pasquini

Senior Lecturer, Department of Learning Technologies, University of North Texas; and Researcher, The Digital Learning and Social Media Research Group, Royal Roads University, Victoria, British Columbia

The Planting of a Seed

In the summer of 2016, as I was preparing to promote my second book, I realized that my online digital identity needed refreshing. Because of using a "professional" first name of Kathryn for publishing, it meant that people could find me under two names (Kathryn and Katie) online. I also noticed that I had several dormant accounts that needed updating and that some accounts did not include a recent headshot. There were also several new online platforms for academics that I had heard of but had not yet taken the time to investigate. To be honest, it was all a bit overwhelming, and I was not quite sure where to start.

As an academic is inclined to do, I began with research. I looked around to see if there was any guidance about how to go about the process of updating my online identity as a scholar and higher education professional. I read through blog posts to see if anyone had created a list of the places that academics typically represented themselves online. I searched through *The Chronicle of Higher Education* and *Inside Higher Ed* to find articles about online identity management for academics. Unfortunately, I did not find much. Fortunately, that experience planted the seed for this book.

Without much guidance, I took a long weekend and got to work finding and updating my accounts and profiles across the Internet. I changed my name to be consistently "Katie Linder" on all my profiles. I uploaded new profile pictures to make myself easier to identify across multiple platforms. I started to think more strategically about how and where I wanted to post regular updates about my scholarship and other "outputs" from my academic life, such as the podcast that I host for my job and the three other podcasts I host on the side. That long weekend served as a good jump start for me, but it also got me thinking about what it means to be an academic online. I found myself reflecting on several questions that became central to this book:

- What do I hope to achieve through my online professional identity?
- To what degree should my online presence be professional? To what degree should it be personal?
- Where should I "be" online? Do I need to have profiles on every platform?
- Whom do I want to connect with through the online platforms where I have profiles and posts? Why do I want to connect with them?
- How much is too much in terms of what I post about my own professional work, publications, and accomplishments?
- How do I engage online in an active way without it taking too much of my time, resources, or energy?

These questions also serve as illustrative examples of the uncertainty I have encountered from many academics who are trying to navigate online spaces in a professional capacity. After I started my own process of updating, I began to have conversations with colleagues and found that many of us are not sure what, who, where, why, and how we should be online as professionals in higher education.

For example, at a recent conference I attended, I was live-tweeting the event (more about live-tweeting in chapter 8). I got to talking with some colleagues about Twitter over lunch and one woman expressed concern about all the negativity online. She thought that if she posted about her life or work in online environments, she would be met primarily with critiques. Instead, she preferred to remain mostly anonymous online, creating accounts where she could "lurk" without anyone knowing who she was. The more we talked, the clearer it became that she was not aware of the depth of community that is now online for higher education professionals looking to connect with and support one another. She felt, in a word, afraid to be actively engaging online. To be sure, "trolls" exist (more about this in chapter 10), but there are also a range of benefits that an online presence can offer for academics and higher education professionals. If you are looking to network, share your work, learn about new ideas and innovations, and/or develop new professional relationships that can lead to collaborations, job offers, and more, then being online is becoming more and more essential.

Talking with this colleague was a helpful reminder for me because I recognized her feeling of fear. I felt that same emotion when I started exploring online platforms and deciding where I wanted to be present online. In the past year, I have talked with many other higher education professionals—of all generations, I think it is important to say—who are also unsure, insecure, and embarrassed about all that they do not know about how to be online. Perhaps this should not be surprising. As DiPiazza (2012) explains in *Friend Me! 600 Years of Social Networking in America,* a book on social networking aimed at young adults, "Every advance in networking technology has met with human fears" (p. 7). This makes sense when you consider that, at its core, online social networking is all about exploring the unknown while simultaneously placing yourself into the most public space imaginable. Indeed, before the Internet, some academics may have shared their ideas with very niche and obscure communities where one's article might have been read by only a handful of colleagues; now it can be presented to millions of people with the click of a mouse.

Although I certainly do not profess to know everything about what it means to be a professional in online environments, I have spent the past year and a half talking with other academics and higher education professionals about these issues. I have reflected deeply about what it means to be online in a professional capacity. I have read what others in academia have said about online engagement, and I have also looked to sources outside of academia such as marketing, business, and philosophy to gain additional perspectives. Early on, I downloaded some podcasts that used that dreaded word *branding* and, somewhat surprisingly, found some very helpful guidance. I also read blogs and books written for creative entrepreneurs and gleaned useful tips and tactics. I spent time researching platform and features tutorials to see what the best practices are for representing yourself online and I tried out many of these ideas in a range of online spaces.

What all this searching, questioning, and thinking has helped me see is that, at the most basic level, if you are a current or aspiring higher education professional, intentionally shaping your digital identity is becoming a career necessity. As Fertik and Thompson (2015), authors of *The Reputation Economy*, point out, "There's no way to be 'off the grid' online" (p. 61). Although we may not want to admit it, the current professional climate is such that if you are not deliberate about your digital presence, you are giving up a pretty significant form of professional currency.

At the same time, the process of being a professional online is becoming increasingly overwhelming. Many of the academics and higher education professionals I have talked with do not know where to start when it comes to launching or revising their online presence. The task seems so big and, without clear guidance, it can be easier to put your head in the digital sand. To make things more complex, new platforms are launching all the time and existing platforms release new features constantly. During the writing of this book, for example, Instagram released its new "Stories" feature where users can post short videos that are available for consumption during a short window of time. This feature is similar to another platform, Snapchat, where users can also share videos and images that then self-destruct a few seconds after they are viewed. This new release created an overlap in the features of Instagram and Snapchat that caused some users to abandon Snapchat and focus solely on their Instagram profiles. Others decided to stay on both platforms. Others used Snapchat for videos and Instagram only for static images. And another group completely ignored the new feature altogether—they had never opened a Snapchat profile to begin with and did not really care about the new feature. Whatever their choices, users had to decide how to integrate the new Instagram feature into their current existence online. This kind of decision-making has become a constant. As new platforms and features launch, we are now continually asked to decide where and how we want to be online. Our online presence should not be—and really cannot be—static.

And so, for the last year and a half, I have been experimenting and, through that experimentation, I have been learning. In addition to the "refresh" that I completed in the summer of 2016, I began to write a weekly essay series that I released through a MailChimp e-mail newsletter and a group blogging platform called Medium. I re-engaged with some platforms I had previously left behind (namely, Facebook and Google+) to see how they had changed over time. I purchased a social media management platform to see how much time I could save by automating some of my posts and whether it might impact the level of engagement I had with other academics (more on this and the issues and controversies around social media scheduling in chapter 8). I started to pay a little more attention to the stats and metrics on various social media platforms to better understand what people were drawn to when I posted news items or images, shared links, and responded to others' questions. And, perhaps most importantly, I intentionally began to engage in social media via regular posts on Instagram and Twitter (my platforms of choice) to see what it meant, and what the benefits were, to "be" online. In other words, I chose to purposefully live my digital identity.

The lessons that I learned and the questions that this process raised for me are embedded throughout this book. I hope that it will serve as a helpful starting point for others who are also thinking about what it means to be online as an academic and higher education professional. You should read this book if you

- care about how others see you online,
- think that digital identities matter,
- believe that your online identity can shape your future opportunities,
- feel overwhelmed by the idea of creating or revising your online identity,
- are not sure how you want to represent yourself online,
- want a comprehensive guide to setting up your online profiles,
- need an overview of where you can establish a professional identity online as a higher education professional,
- are about to go on the job market, or
- are struggling to promote your scholarship or accomplishments as a higher education professional.

Whether you need to build an online identity from scratch, touch up already existing profiles, or overhaul your entire digital representation, this book is for you. That said, where and how you choose to be online is just that—a choice. And it is a very personal one. Some people may not want to engage online at all (although I doubt they have picked up this book). However you choose to build your online identity is completely up to you. I wrote this book because it was something that I needed and could not find. I wrote it so that others can feel more confident about being online as professionals and can make more informed choices about where and how to be in online spaces, and also because I do not want anyone to have limited choices just because they do not know how to get started.

As your academic digital identity continues to evolve and change, thank you for including this book on your journey.

Katie Linder

ACKNOWLEDGMENTS

I wrote this book more publicly than any other project I've previously worked on, and that means that I have a *lot* of people to thank. To everyone who followed along and cheered my progress in my December 2016 writing retreat, my April 2017 writing challenge, and my May 2017 writing retreat, I so appreciate your kind words of encouragement.

During the writing of this book, I also released a podcast (*The Anatomy of a Book*) about my writing experience. Thanks to all the folks who downloaded and listened, followed along with the book's progress, and encouraged my writing process from the sidelines.

I had several engaging conversations as this book was being created. Thanks in particular to Kirsten Behling, Erica Curry, Laurie Maynell, and Brooke Robertshaw. Many others also talked with me about their own experiences and passed along relevant resources in person and on social media. The #acdigid Twitter group was always an inspiration during the drafting of this book.

Thanks to the members of my mastermind group—Josie Ahlquist, Barbi Honeycutt, Michelle Miller, Chavella Pittman, and Tom Tobin—for supporting me through many projects, including the writing of this book, in our monthly phone chats.

A huge thanks to all my colleagues at Oregon State University Extended Campus who asked about and supported the writing of this book even though it was a "side project" to my day-to-day work and occurred in the early mornings, lunch hours, nights, and weekends. I specifically want to thank Lisa Templeton for her support of my writing and projects; Amy Donley and Mary Ellen Dello Stritto for always making me look forward to Monday mornings; and the Ecampus leadership team including Alfonso Bradoch, Claire Cross, Jessica Dupont, Dianna Fisher, and Shannon Riggs—I've learned so much about what it means to be a professional in higher education from each of you.

This book would not be the same without the many profiles of colleagues that I was able to include throughout each of the chapters. Many thanks to Maha Bali, Liz Covant, Monica Cox, Josh Eyler, Laura Gogia, Cathy Hannabach, Natalie Houston, Jeff Jackson, Kevin Kelly, Sara Langworthy, Meggin McIntosh, Jennifer Polk, John Robertson, Bonni Stachowiak, Tom Tobin, and George Veletsianos for graciously agreeing to interviews and for reviewing their profiles for accuracy. Your stories make this book come alive.

I appreciate so much the honesty of the contributors to chapter 10 who shared their stories about responding to online conflict. These faculty, whom I chose to keep anonymous to protect their privacy, taught me what it means to be resilient in online spaces. Special thanks also to John Burkhardt, Josh Knudson, and Mike Wark for speaking with me about institutional responses to online conflict aimed at faculty members.

Much gratitude also to each contributor in the conclusion. Lee Skallerup Bessette, Kevin Gannon, and an anonymous colleague were each so generous about sharing their perspectives of what it means to be an academic professional online. It's a privilege to know you all.

A huge thanks to Laura Pasquini for writing the book's foreword, for introducing me to the #acdigid community, for sharing several useful resources throughout the drafting process, and for cheering my progress along the way.

As always, thanks to Mom and Craig, Ralph and Judy, Dad and Peggy, Beth and Matt, Megan and Brett, my five nieces and nephews, and my incredibly supportive Gram and Grandpa. I always appreciated when you asked about this book's progress in the midst of your own incredibly busy lives.

From the very beginning of this book, my partner was a constant cheerleader. He knew I could do it when I wasn't sure myself, he cleared an incredible amount of space for this book in both of our lives, and he offered consulting on some of the more technical components of the book's content. Once again, I couldn't have done it without you, Ben.

INTRODUCTION
Why Digital Identities Matter

The Current Digital Landscape

In higher education, professional online identities have become increasingly important for building and maintaining reputation. A rightly (or wrongly, for that matter) worded tweet can cause an academic blog post to go viral. When this happens, the author can become "known" for something that may have been relatively tangential to his or her work, and sometimes with a negative effect. Take as just one example the blog post that came out in August 2016 in which author Gabriel Egan "laments the narcissistic craving for others' approval" (Egan, 2016) brought on by social media engagement. The response to this post was swift, particularly on Twitter, where many academics argued for the benefits of social media engagement, including the ways in which social media creates a space for diversity and inclusivity in academia. Egan is a Shakespeare scholar, but for the week that this post was passed around social media, his words were read and debated by academics from many disciplines and, perhaps, were interpreted quite differently from what he intended.

An academic professional online presence—whether through social media engagement with students, communicating with colleagues via e-mail or discussion boards, or creating profiles to share research and teaching artifacts—has become a central part of many of our daily lives. Ironically, given the importance of digital identities to job searches, the promotion and distribution of scholarly work, pedagogical innovation, and many other components of an academic life, higher education professionals receive little to no training about how to best represent themselves in a digital space.

Currently, almost two-thirds of Americans own a smartphone (A. Smith, 2015) and the majority of adults in the United States (68%) are Facebook users. In addition, 28% of U.S. adults are on Instagram, 26% on Pinterest, 25% on LinkedIn, and 21% on Twitter; more than half of U.S. adults who are online (56%) use more than one of these five platforms (Greenwood, Perrin, & Duggan, 2016). U.S. adults with some college experience are more likely to use social media than those with a high school degree or less, and the majority of Whites (65%), Hispanics (65%), and African Americans (56%) use social media (Perrin, 2015). Online engagement has become intricately tied to one's use of social media platforms. Usability statistics from some of the more popular social media and media sharing sites provide clear evidence of the pervasiveness of these online environments, as evident in the following examples from five popular online platforms—Facebook, YouTube, Instagram, LinkedIn, and Twitter (for definitions of each, see the glossary in the back of the book).

Facebook

Facebook is America's most popular social networking platform, with 79% of online Americans now using it (Greenwood et al., 2016). The platform has 1.18 billion daily active users on average and 1.79 billion monthly active users (as of September 2016), including over 1 billion users on mobile devices ("Stats," 2016). Approximately 84.9% of Facebook's daily active users are outside the United States and Canada ("Stats," 2016).

YouTube

YouTube has over one billion users and hundreds of millions of hours of video are watched daily, generating billions of views ("Statistics," 2016). The platform reaches more 18- to 34- and 18- to 49-year-olds than any cable network in the United States, with more than half of views from mobile devices ("Statistics," 2016).

Instagram

Instagram has more than 600 million members (as of December 2016); of those, 100 million joined in just the past 6 months ("600 Million and Counting," 2016). Users on the platforms have shared over 40 billion photos, at an average of 95 million photos and videos each day (Parker, 2016).

LinkedIn

LinkedIn currently has more than 467 million registered members in over 200 countries and territories ("About Us," 2016). New members sign up on LinkedIn at a rate of more than two new members per second and there are more than 40 million students and recent college graduates on LinkedIn, making them LinkedIn's fastest-growing demographic ("About Us," 2016).

Twitter

Twitter has over 313 million active monthly users, with 82% of active users on mobile and 79% of accounts outside of the United States ("Twitter Usage," 2016).

Digital Confusion

Although one might think that with this many people online we would all know where and how to be in these spaces, but this is just not the case. We continue to question the value and purpose of various online spaces and digital platforms. Among other things, we want to know how being online benefits us personally and professionally. What does it mean to "be" online? How much time should we devote to our digital selves? What do we have control over regarding our online representation? Why should we bother spending our time and energy on developing and maintaining an online presence? And, given that "each platform is unique, and requires a unique formula" (Vaynerchuk, 2013, p. 14), how can we ever be assured that what we are doing online is correct or that we are using platforms in the best way possible?

To be sure, being online is not easy. Online spaces are both complicated and vulnerable. Because platforms, features, and rules of engagement keep changing, even social media experts do not know what they are doing half the time. Indeed, Jessie Daniels, in an interview for the collection *The Digital Academic* (Mewburn, 2017), states: "Right now, it's very much there are no rules, there are no guidelines, there are just a few examples and some cautionary tales. There aren't really guidelines or a set of best practices" (p. 167). If you feel some discomfort being in online environments, it may be for one of the following reasons:

- *It is necessarily social and public.* Online social spaces are inherently vulnerable for many people who view digital spaces as just another place where they might face rejection. Being online is about being yourself, but being yourself in any space can be hard. With "friends" and "followers" as public metrics, it can be difficult to enter digital spaces with confidence. People may or may not engage with the content that you are sharing online. Despite their best efforts to the contrary, many people struggle to separate out the metrics of online engagement from their own personal worth. (For more on building and engaging with community online, see chapter 9.)
- *It means you might fail.* By putting yourself out there online, you are asking for people to engage with you and your ideas. There will probably come a time where you might say something that you later regret. Given the changing nature of platforms and features, it is also inevitable that you will engage in an online platform in a way that demonstrates your lack of knowledge of the cultural norms. So much of digital engagement is learned through experimentation, and failure is a necessary part of experimentation.
- *It requires awareness of constant change.* New platforms and features are available regularly and digital spaces go out of style and require you to transition your time and energy elsewhere (remember MySpace?). The digital world is in constant flux, so part of engaging online means being willing to try new things, being open to change, and paying attention to the latest developments and trends.
- *It requires an investment of time.* Being online means being in relationships with others and, just like in our face-to-face encounters, this takes time and emotional energy. In addition to learning the "formulas" of each platform, we each need to decide how and how much to engage in each of the online spaces where we choose to be.

But, as many of us are well aware, being online also provides a lot of benefits:

- *You can build a network.* Nurturing digital relationships and curating content online is an investment that can have huge payoffs in job opportunities, collaborations, and learning about new resources for work (see some examples of this in the conclusion). You can meet and engage with people from all over the world and you never know where those connections will lead.

- *You can more easily share ideas with a broad audience.* It has never been easier to share your work in open platforms where it can be found by people all over the world. You can post content in a range of mediums from text based, to images, to video, and more. Perhaps most importantly, you can receive feedback on this content from a wide range of people in real time.
- *You can be seen as an expert.* By consistently posting quality content on a particular subject, you can become an expert online in a relatively short amount of time. Although academics are used to years of commitment to receive degrees that signal expertise, online expertise is significantly quicker to earn.
- *You have more information at your fingertips.* Although it can be overwhelming, we have more information available to us than ever before. Connecting and sharing information with colleagues online can make our jobs easier, our research stronger, and our work more efficient.

The Digital Landscape in Higher Education

Although recent studies have found that faculty use social media more for their personal lives than they do professionally (Moran, Seaman, & Tinti-Kane, 2012; Seaman & Tinti-Kane, 2013), faculty use of social media for personal, professional, and teaching purposes is increasing over time (Seaman & Tinti-Kane, 2013). Faculty reticence to use social media in a professional capacity may stem, in part, from concerns about other faculty who have been attacked on social media (see more about responding to online conflict in chapter 10). A 2015 *Inside Higher Ed* survey found that 60% of instructors agree or strongly agree that they are concerned about attacks on professors for comments on social media. Indeed, most of the faculty members surveyed (75%) do not use social media to discuss their scholarship or their political views. Interestingly, this same survey also found that faculty members are not sure about whether social media is a good way for scholars to communicate with the broader public; approximately equal numbers agree (35%) and disagree (36%) (Straumsheim, Jaschik, & Lederman, 2015).

These concerns are not unfounded. Recently, *The Chronicle of Higher Education* covered the story of a professor who was fired for comments that he made on his personal Twitter account when he posited that Hurricane Harvey was "karma" in response to Texas being a majority Republican-voting state (Turnage, 2017). These kinds of stories, however rare that they may be, strengthen the urban-legend-like qualities of the cautions faculty and higher education professionals might receive about engaging online. These stories emphasize that it can be hard to know where the land mines are and how best to avoid them.

However, trade publications like *The Chronicle of Higher Education* and *Inside Higher Ed* also regularly feature blog posts with topics including "How to Tailor

Your Online Image" (Kelsky, 2016), "Manage Your Digital Identity" (Meyers, 2013), "How to Build a Following on Twitter" (Jenkins, 2016), and "Why You May Need Social Media for Your Career" (Warner, 2016). Indeed, there is a growing, and needed, literature regarding the engagement of academics and higher education professionals online. Books like *Social Media for Academics* (Carrigan, 2016) and *Social Media for Educators* (Joosten, 2012) provide how-to guides for engaging online as a researcher and teacher, respectively. In higher education, whether we are ready or not, the digital age has arrived and is here to stay.

Setting aside the broad array of scholarship on integrating technology into teaching and pedagogy, which is too vast to cover here, the remaining literature in this area can be broadly categorized into the following main topics: academic blogging, social media engagement for professional purposes, academics' and higher education professionals' lived experiences online, and the use of altmetrics from online channels as a measurement for scholarly impact.

Academic Blogging

Blogs, short for web logs, have become a popular form for academic online engagement to the degree that some have argued that "academic blogging can and should have an acknowledged place in the overall ecology of scholarship" (Maitzen, 2012, p. 348). A quick review of the blogging literature finds articles on blogging as a public intellectual (Kirkup, 2010), blogging as social practice (Davies & Merchant, 2006), blogging as community of practice (Mewburn & Thompson, 2013), blogging as a form of academic scholarship (Powell, Jacob, & Chapman, 2012), blogging as a pedagogical practice (Nackerud & Scaletta, 2008), and blogging and identity formation (Estes, 2012). Scholars write about blogs that are disciplinarily situated in the humanities (Davies & Merchant, 2006; Lindemann, 2010; Maitzen, 2012), law (Hurt & Yin, 2006; Solum, 2006), and the sciences (Mahrt & Puschmann, 2014; Riesch & Mendel, 2014).

Academics have been found to use blogs for a wide range of purposes. Kjellberg (2010) argues that academic bloggers write to share, be creative, and find connection. Mewburn and Thompson (2013) categorized 100 academic blogs into nine main content areas: self-help, descriptions of academic practices, technical advice, academic culture critique, research dissemination, career advice, personal reflections, information, and teaching advice, with the two most common areas being academic cultural critique and research dissemination. Although there is no way to tell how many academic blogs exist or how many academic or higher education professionals are engaging in blogging, the emerging literature demonstrates that blogging is becoming a standardized academic practice.

Social Media Engagement

Perhaps not too surprisingly, much of the literature surrounding social media engagement in academia is related to the use of different tools in the online and face-to-face classroom (see, e.g., Bosch, 2009; Farmer, Yue, & Brooks, 2008; Seaman &

Tinti-Kane, 2013; Yensen, 2012). However, the literature on faculty and higher education professionals' use of different online platforms is beginning to grow. Although some of this literature focuses on the rationales for academics to use social media (see, e.g., Miah, 2016) much of the literature looks at engagement with specific social media platforms such as Twitter (Ross, Terras, Warwick, & Welsh, 2011; Veletsianos, 2012), Facebook (Roblyer, McDaniel, Webb, Herman, & Witty, 2010), Academia .edu and ResearchGate (Duffy & Pooley, 2017; Ovadia, 2014; Thelwall & Kousha, 2014; Yu, Wu, Alhalabi, Kao, & Wu, 2016), Google Scholar (Harzing, 2017), and Pinterest (Dudenhoffer, 2012). A Pew Research study also found that "incorporating social media into the research workflow can improve the overall responsiveness and timeliness of scholarly communication. It also has a powerful secondary advantage: exposing and pinpointing scholarly processes once hidden and ephemeral" (Brown, Cowan, & Green, 2016, n.p.).

Academics and higher education professionals are in need of resources for how to share their work and better understand online processes as new online spaces materialize and mature. Practical guides such as Carrigan's (2016) share concrete steps for how to use social media for publicizing academic work, building a network, engaging the public, and managing information. Additional resources have also emerged to help academics and higher education professionals share work with the broader public through traditional and digital media (Gasman, 2016; Tyson, 2010). Exploratory research in this area is also growing; for example, Al-Aufi and Fulton (2014) have studied how social media tools are used for informal scholarly communication. More recently, Veletsianos and Shaw (2017) examined how the engagement of scholars online is impacted by the imagined audiences that academics believe they will encounter.

Academics' and Higher Education Professionals' Lived Experiences Online

As more academics and higher education professionals are engaging online across social media and other professional platforms, literature has emerged to study their experiences. Barbour and Marshall (2012) provide a five-part framework for how academics present themselves online as formal, networked, comprehensive, teaching, and uncontainable. Interestingly, these different personas can be navigated both within and outside of institutional settings. Barbour and Marshall also found that "the level of identity planning and management varies among individuals, and quite dramatically over the course of an academic year." One significant aspect of this framework is how fluid it can be, depending on time of year, online platform, and context, among other variables.

Scholars have also explored such topics as how academics participate online as researchers (Costa, 2014; Daniels, 2013; Marwick, Blackwell, & Lo, 2016), how the digital world is shaping knowledge flow and gatekeeping in the academy (Graham, 2013), how online engagement impacts tenure and promotion (Gruzd, Staves, & Wilk, 2011), how online engagement affects academic reputation (Reich, 2011), how the nature of student and faculty engagement together online has changed (Malesky

& Peters, 2012), and how higher education professionals engage in social networking online (Veletsianos & Kimmons, 2013). A short perusal of the literature uncovers these and many other fascinating topics (for helpful collections of this literature, see also Lupton, Mewburn, & Thompson, 2017; Veletsianos, 2016a).

Altmetrics

Alternative metrics, called *altmetrics,* involve the use of information from social media to measure the impact of scholarly work. For example, rather than only measuring traditional citation rates, altmetrics might also consider how frequently a piece of scholarly work was tweeted about or otherwise shared on social media. Priem, Piwowar, and Hemminger (2012) describe several "events" that might be counted in altmetrics, including Wikipedia links to articles, social bookmarking through web services such as Mendeley, Twitter links, and links from blog posts, as well as Facebook likes, clicks, shares, and comments, among many other metrics.

Still relatively new in the digital landscape, altmetrics are a contested space. For one thing, altmetrics are hard to define and even harder to measure. Although some scholars represent altmetrics as the new normal (see Taylor, 2013), others question whether altmetrics work at all. Indeed, Thelwall, Haustein, Larivière, and Sugimoto (2013) have demonstrated that the usefulness of altmetrics is highly dependent on platform and effects of time. Eysenbach (2011) argues that altmetrics should be used to complement more traditional citation impact measures.

How altmetrics can be useful to scholars is also still under debate. For example, some scholars list social media engagements on a CV, but this is by no means a standardized practice. New tools such as Impactstory (https://impactstory.org) have emerged to help scholars more automatically generate altmetrics, but many of these tools are still relatively young. Impactstory utilizes ORCID, which creates a persistent digital identifier for scholars to track online engagements with a particular individual's work. Similarly, a tool called Altmetric (www.altmetric.com) depends heavily on the use of a publication's digital object identifier, or DOI.

As more scholars engage with and promote their work on social media platforms, the altmetric landscape will continue to evolve. As additional definitions, tools, and services become available, further experimentation will continue to clarify the altmetrics landscape.

Why Digital Identities Matter

Some would argue that playing this new digital game is not worth our time and energy. Others would contend that spending 7 to 10 years on advanced degrees is also not worth it. And yet many of us have done just that. We invested time, energy, money, and emotional effort in earning pieces of paper that call us experts in niche fields. Digital identities matter for the same reasons that our academic credentials matter. In our professional lives, many of us are playing a similar game about credibility, networking, and getting ahead. Our degrees act as one way that we can open doors for ourselves and be eligible for certain professional experiences that others are not "qualified" to do. By "mastering" our subjects and becoming "experts" we are following well-established rules and traditions of academia. In the same way that we leverage our formal credentials, we can also learn to leverage our digital credentials. Just as we had to learn the language and customs of higher education, being a successful professional online means learning the language, customs, and strategies of institutions like social media.

As much as it might seem to the contrary, this book is about more than online platforms and tools. This is a book about who you are as a professional. It is about who you have been in the past, who you are now, and who you will be in the future. For that reason, I intend for this book to be as much a "how-to-be-online" guide as it is a "how-to-be-yourself" reflective experience. The more you know about who you want to be and why, the easier it will be to engage in online spaces. Although I would never argue that there is a solidified and permanent "you" that needs to be signified online, I do believe that there is a "you-as-you-are-now" that does require a form of representation in digital spaces.

As this book demonstrates, I have also come to believe that being online as a professional in higher education has become a necessity. However, others disagree. In a piece for the *New York Times*, productivity writer and computer science professor Cal Newport (2016) advises, "If you're serious about making an impact in the world, power down your smartphone, close your browser tabs, roll up your sleeves and get to work." To a degree, Newport is right. Engaging online can be a distracting, time-intensive hobby (this is something the anonymous contributor in the conclusion might also agree with). But, as I show throughout this book, when done with purpose, it can also lead to professional opportunities and relationships to which you might not otherwise have been exposed.

A Few Words on Language

There are several terms that I use consistently throughout this book that may need a little explanation. *Social media* refers to specific kinds of online platforms (Twitter, Facebook, Instagram, LinkedIn, and others) that are specifically built to create community, to encourage conversation, and to provide digital social spaces. *Social networking* describes the actions of people who engage on social media sites. Although *social networking* is also a broader term that can describe interactions that occur in face-to-face environments (e.g., the work of Christakis & Fowler, 2009), in this book it is used to refer to digital interactions via social media platforms. *Academics* primarily refers to faculty members (including contingent faculty) who are teaching, researching, and publishing in the field of higher education. I chose a broad term intentionally so that this phrasing was as inclusive as possible. *Higher education professionals* includes the range of people within the field of higher education who are not faculty members but who are in need of a professional online identity. This group includes administrators in all areas such as student affairs, academic affairs, instructional technology, faculty development, faculty leadership, and other areas of colleges and universities. I frequently use the combination term *academics and higher education professionals* to try to be as inclusive as possible when talking about the potential readers of this book. Please note that there is also a comprehensive glossary included at the end of the book for terms, platforms, features, and other vocabulary mentioned throughout.

How to Use This Book

Like many other components of our academic lives such as designing courses, revising scholarship, or effectively leading committees, managing your online identity is an iterative process. Although I wish I could say different, it is not a task that you will check off your list and never return to again. However, I also think it is the iterative nature of online identity development and updating that is a large part of what makes this process both creative and fun. I hope that you will revisit the activities in this book as frequently as needed to refresh your online identity when you choose to go on the job market, when you need to promote a new piece of scholarship, or when you want to emphasize a new professional skill set that you have developed.

Writing a book on managing your academic identity online when the online environment is constantly changing has its challenges. To ensure that this book would not be obsolete before it was even published, I decided to keep the content in the book focused on you, the reader, and the choices that you will need to make about your professional identity online. Many of these choices, as you will see, are not about the platforms or the features available to you. Rather, they are about your values, your professional aspirations, and how much time and energy you are willing to invest in managing your online identity. Throughout this book, there are a series of reflective questions and activities to guide you as you self-evaluate and revise your professional online identity. The book will be most useful to you if you take the time to answer the questions provided, peruse the examples, and explore the additional readings that are recommended. Although I do offer some basic overviews of platforms and features (see, e.g., chapters 2 and 8), I have designed the book as a guide that is, for the most part, platform agnostic.

To offer you more detailed information related to the technology elements discussed throughout the book, including tutorials on different platforms, you can look to the book's bonus features available online. The book has a companion website at www.mypiobook.com, where you will find audio extras, PDF handouts, a syllabus example for how to use the book as a course text, additional examples, links, tutorials, and a range of other resources. There are also directions in specific chapters to go to the companion website when there are relevant bonus resources so that you will always know when to look for these extra components. If there are additional resources that you would like to see created for the book, I welcome you to contact me at contact@katielinder.work to share your feedback.

Before you read this book, I encourage you to first take a moment to consider the main questions or concerns that you have about revising your academic identity online and write them down in the space provided:

1. _____

   _____

2. _____

   _____

3. _____

If you are you concerned about the time it will take to revise and manage your online identity, you might want to pay particular attention to chapters 4 and 5, which focus on time-management practices.

If you are wondering about how to prioritize where to be online and how to represent yourself, you should make sure to read chapters 2 and 8, which focus specifically on choosing the right platforms and posting appropriate content for each.

If you are unsure about what makes an online academic identity "professional," I would recommend that you start at the beginning with chapters 1 and 3, which both describe the components that make a strong professional online identity and how to self-evaluate what you already have online.

If you are most interested in learning about the tools, strategies, and tactics that will help you level up your online identity game, make sure to read chapters 6, 7, and 11, which are all about specific ways to promote yourself and your work in online environments.

If you are looking for some tips and strategies to more effectively engage with or start new online communities, turn to chapter 9.

If you are concerned about how best to respond to online conflict, whether that is aimed at yourself or your colleagues, turn to chapter 10.

If you want to hear about other academic and higher education professionals' experiences creating their own online identities, read the profiles throughout the book and then turn to the conclusion, where several colleagues share their stories.

This book will give you some of the tools and strategies that you need to be successful. It will explain some of the common "rules" of the game and help you to decide whether you want to play by those rules. It will describe how being online is always about choices that you need to make about the boundaries between your personal and professional lives, your career goals, and the alignment of your online self with your professional values. Whatever brings you to reading this book, I hope that you find it to be a helpful guide as you embark on this professional development journey. Please connect with me and share your experiences managing your online identity through one of the following platforms:

- **Twitter**: @katie__linder (two underscores)
- **Instagram**: katie_linder (one underscore)
- **E-mail**: contact@katielinder.work

I

WHAT MAKES A STRONG DIGITAL IDENTITY?

Digital Curb Appeal

When you search for an academic or higher education professional online, think about what attracts and propels you to engage with various online profiles. What makes you want to "follow" or "friend" someone? For example, you might be attracted to the following:

- A profile that tells you with certainty that you have found the person you are looking for
- A profile that is being maintained with up-to-date information
- A profile that includes enough information that you can find what you need
- A profile that is aesthetically pleasing
- A profile sharing recent information that is of interest to you

Think of someone you know online who has a platform that embodies each of these things. What else do they provide through their online digital identity that draws you in? What makes you want to peruse their previous posts or explore the pages of their profiles or website?

Sometimes, when thinking about what makes a strong digital identity, it can be easier to think about what does *not* make a strong digital identity. For example, you might be repelled by any of the following:

- A profile that does not include a visual representation, so you are not sure if you have found the right person
- An out-of-date profile that has not been recently updated
- An empty or bare-bones profile that has clearly been abandoned
- A profile that is using clashing color choices, that is difficult to read, or that contains errors or typos
- A profile with outdated fonts or other dated design elements (e.g., dancing hamsters or music playing in the background when you visit the site)

Think of someone you know whose online platform repels you. In addition to the components listed, what else about their online identity pushes you away or offers a negative impression?

For good or for bad, a strong digital identity has a lot to do with appearances. In some ways, you can think about your professional online identity as similar to the curb appeal of a house when you put it on the market for sale. Like curb appeal, having a strong online professional identity is all about taking pride in how you are representing yourself to the world. Your online professional identity could be seen by anyone, anywhere, at any time. Indeed, having an online professional identity is the equivalent of always being "on the market" because people can review the information you post at any time. You will always want to make sure that you are representing your best self online for the world to see—especially because what goes on the Internet stays on the Internet. At the very least, you will want to have the equivalent of a well-manicured lawn and some nice hanging flower baskets.

The more that you can identify what you like about—and what pushes you away from—online profiles, the better you will be able to create a compelling online presence for yourself. Take some time to look through the profiles that you like in various online platforms. Start by looking at LinkedIn, Facebook, Instagram, ResearchGate, Academia.edu, Twitter, or other places where you are already a member. If you are not engaged in those platforms, you can look at the institutional web pages of colleagues in your field or check out the professional websites of academics or higher education professionals (mine is www.katielinder.work if you want to start there). As you look through these profiles, note the following:

1. What are the elements that I like or that I am drawn to?

   _____

   _____

   _____

   _____

   _____

2. What are the elements that I do not like or that repel me?

   _____

   _____

   _____

   _____

   _____

The Components of Your Digital Identity

There are several components that make up your digital identity and that we will explore throughout this book. To get started, consider the following foundational components.

Headshot

What image are you using to represent yourself online? By looking at your headshot, people should be able to recognize you across a range of digital platforms. This means that your headshot should be a current, close-up shot of your head and shoulders. A consistent avatar (a representative icon or figure) can also be used, but this should also match your overall digital messaging about your professional life. For example, if you are an entomologist, then using an insect to represent yourself might make sense. (See Box 1.1 for a common question about putting your image online.)

Bio Statement

Almost anywhere that you exist online will offer an option to include a bio statement. These will be of varying lengths (Twitter will be shorter; LinkedIn will be longer) and should be crafted based on the platform and what audience will be engaging with the bio statements. (More about how to draft effective bio statements in chapter 4.)

Personal Brand

Academics do not often think about their identities as personal brands, so another way to think about your academic brand is the reputation that you are trying to build. Consider the following questions:

BOX 1.1.

Should you put your picture online?

Talking with a range of academics and higher education professionals, I was somewhat surprised by how many people were nervous about sharing images of themselves online. Some people felt that sharing images would result in a lack of privacy. Others were concerned about the images being used without their consent. Additional concerns were raised about identity theft and also about discrimination, particularly by women and people of color. All are valid issues to raise when considering what to post online.

As you consider what image(s) to post, you might want to start by searching your name via Google or another search platform to see what images already exist of you online. The range of images already online might surprise you.

Although I recommend, at minimum, posting an up-to-date professional headshot when you create profiles online that are tied to your work, this is not mandatory. You need to make sure that you are comfortable with what you are posting online to represent yourself and those decisions are entirely up to you. That said, keep in mind that if you choose not to post any images, it may be difficult for people to recognize that you are the person they are looking for if they attempt to find and connect with you online.

- What do you want to be known for?
- What do you want your colleagues to say about you (in a positive way) when you are not present?
- What kinds of things about your professional life and accomplishments will draw people to you?
- What do you consider yourself to be an expert in?

All of these questions can help you to shape the kinds of information that you will share online (more about this is also covered in chapter 4; see also Box 1.2 for one example of how a higher education professional shapes his brand online).

Online Content

Any time that you write a status update, blog post, or other online offering, it becomes part of the online content of your digital identity. This includes any text you create and post, images and videos that you share, or other content that you include on your

BOX 1.2.

Being intentional online.

Kevin Kelly
Higher education consultant

Find Kevin online:
LinkedIn: www.linkedin.com/in/kevin-kelly-26b19a/
Twitter: https://twitter.com/KevinKelly0

When Kevin thinks about his online presence, one keyword comes to mind— *intentionality*. Although his online presence has been evolving over time as he has moved from being institutionally affiliated to working as a freelance consultant, Kevin has always used online platforms like listservs, Twitter, LinkedIn, and Lynda.com to purposefully provide value through offering answers, advice, resources, blog posts, and online courses.

Kevin sees his network as a set of personal relationships, many of which have started offline thanks to working almost 20 years in higher education. He continues to build that network by adding diverse connections who can help him grow professionally and to strengthen it by keeping connections warm through social media and regular check-ins. He still receives many projects via word of mouth, so he does not yet actively use a formal web presence to drum up business.

However, Kevin still strives to be "findable" online. Because of his popular name, he has had to purposefully use his online presence to differentiate himself from others (e.g., the *Wired* magazine founder). He views his online presence as similar to his philosophy on educational technology: The goal comes first; then the technology to achieve that goal follows.

profiles. You will want to make sure that the content you are providing is intentional and aligned with your professional academic identity. Also, most online content is open for anyone to see and it exists forever, so you want to make sure that everything you post is the equivalent of what you would also post on a permanent billboard. (This is discussed further in chapter 8.)

Thinking about each of these areas can seem overwhelming. It is understandable that many academics give up before they even start to shape their online professional identities. In the following section, I offer a way to break down these components through six evaluative categories that will help divide the process of managing your online identity into a reasonable set of tasks. Additional steps to manage your online presence as efficiently as possible are also provided in chapter 5.

Six Criteria of a Strong Digital Identity

To have a strong digital identity, there are six main components that you need to consider (see Figure 1.1). In chapter 3, you will apply each of these criteria to self-evaluate your current digital identity, so what follows are definitions of each criterion, along with some concrete examples from multiple online platforms. The six criteria are consistency, professionalism, accuracy, organization, quality, and representativeness.

Consistency

In *The Reputation Economy*, Fertik and Thompson (2015) argue that "your online and offline worlds [should be] consistent. In the ideal scenario, what's online about you will match who you are in real life" (p. 85). For those new to online profiles, this may serve as somewhat of a relief. All you must do is shape your online identity to look like how you describe yourself and how you act in your real life. Fertik and Thompson (2015) argue that "a consistent message will create a positive cycle of reinforcement: what you say offline matches what they find online, and what they find online matches what you say" (p. 85). This kind of consistency can strengthen your reputation and the kinds of professional skills and values that you are known for.

Figure 1.1. Six criteria of a strong digital identity.

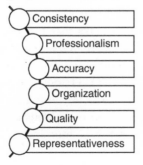

However, others have pointed out that this kind of consistency is challenging given the range of roles that we play in our personal and professional lives. For example, John Scalzi (2016) shares in a blog post on his online versus offline personas that

> it's not (necessarily) insincere or *bad* if your presentation in one medium varies from your presentation in another. Certainly one *can* have a presentation of self that is false or hypocritical, or have such a wide variance between one presentation and the other that it gives the appearance of either (or both). But there's a ways to go before you get to that point. I don't tend to think my presentation in any circumstance is false, although I admit ego and self-interest keeps me from being a perfect observer of me. . . . Hello, I'm a human and that means I'm complicated.

As Scalzi points out, there will always be some variance in our presentations online, particularly given the range of ways that online platforms ask us to present our identities, whether that be via images, posts of 280 characters or less, longer essays, or other forms of information. Identities are complicated in real life so it logically follows that our online identities will have some of the same complexities.

As you consider what degree of consistency you want to include in your online and offline professional lives, ask yourself about your underlying core professional values. If people who interact with you online or in person were to take away just one or two ideas about you, your personality, and your values as a professional, what would you want those ideas to be?

1. _____
   _____
   _____
   _____

2. _____
   _____
   _____
   _____

Keep in mind that it is helpful if, when looking for you online, people can recognize you across platforms because of the consistency that you offer with your online identity. Someone you do not know who looks you up online should be able to, relatively easily, find you in multiple places and feel confident that all those profiles are yours. One of the easiest ways that this can be accomplished is through using a consistent headshot and similar words to represent yourself across platforms. For example, my current bio statements on Twitter, Instagram, and Medium are the same: "author | writer | podcaster @YGT_podcast & @RIA_podcast | list-making enthusiast | passionate about process | learning like it's my job." I also use similar headshots across platforms. One of the main benefits of having an intentional online presence is that it makes you easier to be found when someone is searching for you; consistency plays a key role in this.

Professionalism

How you appear online goes beyond your profile image and content to also include how you interact in various online settings. The safest assumption is that nothing is anonymous online, so your comments, social media posts, and communications should also be considered part of your professional identity and be drafted accordingly. Thinking about how you want to be viewed as a professional can help you decide the kind of balance between personal and professional that you will want to include online. Some considerations about this balance include the following:

- Will you use profanity in posts?
- What kind of humor or sarcasm, if any, will you employ?
- Will you share images of yourself? Your family members?
- To what degree will you allow yourself to be negative online—that is, to what degree will you offer critiques of events, people, products, and so on?
- What are the goals of your digital identity as related to your professional life?
- How do you envision your digital identity contributing to your professional reputation?

Although one might think that these questions will have different responses depending on the current state of your professional life (e.g., whether you are on the job market), it may be a better idea to try to maintain consistency over time so that your online professional identity is a genuine and accurate representation of who you are as a professional over the long term. The Internet does have a history, so when you eventually do go on the job market, start to promote a new piece of scholarship, or begin to form new relationships for a grant proposal, you will want to make sure what people find about you is what you want them to find.

The best example of the importance of professionalism online is probably the job market. It is now a common practice for human resources professionals and hiring managers to conduct a Google search on candidates before advancing them to the interview stage or as part of the references-checking process. Regularly conducting an online search with your own name (or, perhaps more easily, setting up a Google Alert for your name) will help you to see the kinds of things that other people see when they search for you (see Box 1.3 for more information on Google Alerts). Take a moment to conduct this search now and list the top 10 websites that appear when you search for your own name:

1. _____
2. _____
3. _____
4. _____
5. _____
6. _____

7. _____

8. _____

9. _____

10. _____

BOX 1.3.
Google Alerts.

> Through Google, you can set up different "alerts" for words or phrases so that when those particulars are mentioned online, you get notified via e-mail. You might want to set up a Google Alert for your own name, the names of your publications, or other topics or areas of interest where you want to stay up-to-date on new online content. Visit www.google.com/alerts to create the alerts.

Conducting this search every six months or so will give you an ongoing picture of your online presence and whether it is changing over time in ways that are productive for your professional life and career goals.

Accuracy

One of the hardest tasks for academics and higher education professionals with active teaching, research, and service obligations can be keeping online profiles current and accurate. Fertik and Thompson (2015) state that "it should go without saying that the information that's out there about you must be true. Ditch distracting tidbits and remove any exaggerations" (p. 86). Although I agree with their advice, I acknowledge that keeping all your online platforms accurate can be easier said than done. If you are already systematically updating your CV or résumé, then you can just add in regular updates to your online profiles to that schedule. Unfortunately, many of us have a hard time keeping up with accurate CVs and résumés as it is. As you decide how and where to represent yourself online, you will want to ensure that you have only the number of online profiles that you can reasonably update on a regular basis to ensure professionalism and consistency for your online identity (this will be covered in greater detail in chapter 5). We have all gone through the process of Googling a colleague only to find the online representation to be out-of-date, inaccurate, and confusing. It may be unclear how to make contact or to find recent information; it may just appear as if the person is never online and has left certain profiles to grow digital weeds. Keeping your online professional identity accurate is essential to ensuring your digital curb appeal (see Box 1.4 for one of most important online components to keep up-to-date).

As you develop as an academic and higher education professional, it is natural that some of your accomplishments, job experiences, publications, and other career components may become dated or disconnected from your current professional

BOX 1.4.
Keeping your headshot up-to-date.

In addition to making sure that your profiles all include the latest information about your professional experience and accomplishments, accuracy in your visual representation is crucial to ensure the alignment of your online professional identity with who you are in real life. For example, if you have recently lost or gained a significant amount of weight, or changed your hairstyle or colored your hair, or if you have been using a headshot taken a decade ago, you will want to update your headshot to ensure an accurate representation of your current appearance.

goals. This is especially true when you consider the range of things you may have added to your CV or résumé as you were completing graduate school and readying yourself for the job market. Although this information is not technically *inaccurate*, it may be distracting from the areas of your professional life that you want people to be focusing on now. As you look through your online presence with an eye for inaccuracies, also look for these outdated areas that may need a little sprucing up.

Organization

All academics have professional lives that can be categorized and ordered by a range of metrics (e.g., publication type, date of presentation or service obligation, level of course taught, job title). Consider these structures when building an online identity so that information is not offered to viewers as a data dump. Most sites have structures to help with this, but you will also have to make strategic decisions about the order of information that you present and what gets prioritized for your audience. It is entirely possible that different platforms will have information about you prioritized in different ways. Just as you would draft different versions of a cover letter when applying to a range of jobs, you will also need to draft slightly different versions of your online identity to ensure that you are leveraging each platform to its full advantage.

For example, although you may want to put your current and previous positions at the top of your LinkedIn or ResearchGate page, your previous professional experiences may be less relevant to your followers on Twitter (not to mention that those details will not fit in the space allotted for your Twitter profile anyway). You will want to approach each platform you utilize online with a fresh eye to see how best to utilize its features to represent your professional life and accomplishments (more about this will be covered in chapter 2). The easiest way to ensure that your organizational structure is the best possible for each platform is to consider (a) your primary goal for each platform and (b) the platform audience. The way that you organize your information should be aligned with both what you are hoping to accomplish by posting your information to that platform and the needs of the platform audience members who will be engaging with you there.

Quality

How you appear online will immediately tell your audience something about you. Just as we make first impressions in person within a matter of minutes (and, some say, seconds), our online presence also offers viewers a first impression. For example, are you organized, technically savvy, or well networked? Or are you disorganized, technically challenged, with few followers? The quality of the materials you post online and the time you take to create a quality online identity that is consistent, professional, accurate, and organized will pay off in the long run because of the first impression that you offer.

Whether you want it to or not, the quality of your online professional identity can help bring opportunities to your doorstep or it can repel people from contacting you. As a specific example, I was looking online recently to find a possible contributor to an edited volume that I am organizing. The publisher I work with asked for a new chapter to be added to the proposal and it was on a topic that I was less familiar with. I started Googling to see who might be an expert on the topic so that I could reach out to find a possible author for the chapter. There were a couple of different options that immediately rose to the surface of who might work as experts to draft the particular chapter topic I needed. The first was only represented online by an older website that was not up-to-date. It did not include anything that the person had worked on for the previous couple of years and I could not find this person on any other online platforms. Another potential author had an institutional web page that included an updated list of current citations and conference presentations that applied to the chapter topic. Can you guess which one I ultimately contacted and who is now authoring that chapter?

Just as we are careful about the quality of our work that appears in print as a peer-reviewed article, book chapter, conference proceeding, or other publication, we should also be careful that our online presence represents the conscientious professionals we are. Although the Internet can feel more informal and temporary, it is becoming more formal and permanent as the impressions we make have real consequences for our professional lives and career goals.

Representativeness

Each of the criteria mentioned so far when combined result in the sixth criterion of representativeness. Your digital academic identity should offer as complete a picture as you would like to create of your professional self, including all of the major components of your professional experience, skills, and strengths. You may not include everything about your professional life on every platform, but someone who views you across platforms should find that your professional life is aligned across all the representations that you offer. This is particularly important if you have a new accomplishment (job promotion, new job, new book) or a shift in your professional identity (research in a whole new area or a new role with your national organization). For example, when I first started podcasting, I made sure to update my online professional platforms to include this new information about myself. It not only helped

BOX 1.5.
Representing your full self online.

Natalie Houston
Productivity coach
Associate professor of English
University of Massachusetts Lowell

Find Natalie online:
Professional website: http://nmhouston.com
Twitter: https://twitter.com/nmhouston
Blog: www.chronicle.com/blogs/profhacker/author/nhouston

Natalie is a busy academic. In addition to her full-time role as a faculty member, she runs a business on the side. Fortunately, Natalie's passion is productivity. She is a personal productivity coach and regularly writes about productivity as a contributor to *The Chronicle of Higher Education's ProfHoacker* blog.

Given her wide range of professional activities, Natalie is intentional about representing her full identity online. Although her side business is separate from her day job, she finds that her academic credentials are valuable to her coaching clients. Moreover, a cohesive online presence helps Natalie to embrace the connections between her various professional commitments.

Although at one time it might have been appropriate for academics to let their institutions decide where they should be online, Natalie now believes that being a professional online means having a selected online presence that is carefully cultivated and nurtured. She likes to create her own online space through platforms like her personal website and make thoughtful choices about how and where she wants to be online.

For Natalie, her intentional online presence is empowering to all aspects of her professional life and work.

promote my work in this new medium but also showed anyone who tried to find me online that this is an important component of my professional life and identity. (For an example of a higher education professional who intentionally represents her full self online, see Box 1.5.)

Before self-assessing your current online identity, in the following chapter you will learn more about the range of platforms where you might choose to engage online. Then, in chapter 3, you will have the opportunity to self-assess your current online presence across platforms. Chapter 3 will also offer concrete applications for each of the six criteria to the four main components of your digital professional identity (headshot, biography, personal brand, online content).

2

CHOOSING WHERE TO
BE PRESENT ONLINE

The Internet Runs on FOMO

Although the Internet may want us to believe otherwise, you do not actually need to be on all platforms, social media and otherwise, at all times. Obviously, this is impossible to do, but it does not stop most people from trying to keep up with a range of social media sites and profiles. *Fear of missing out* (or FOMO) has become a significant factor in choosing both where and how to engage online. We want to make sure that we are not missing any important opportunities, information, or connections that we could be building on that platform. Although it is certainly true that social media and other online platforms have increased one's potential to be found and followed, to try to keep up with everything at once creates a kind of manic existence. This is, in part, because of the amount of information that is now available 24 hours a day; it is also because of the way that social media and websites operate. The Internet runs on the idea of FOMO; it serves as the fuel that keeps people checking their e-mail and social media first thing in the morning and last thing at night.

In this chapter, I offer an overview of platforms and features so that you can make informed and intentional choices about where you might want to be online as an academic or higher education professional. I do not advocate any one platform or feature as being universally embraced, but rather encourage you to review the platforms and features in this chapter, consider your own career goals and professional values, and decide what you think is best for you.

Platforms and Features

The number of platforms available to academics and higher education professionals can feel overwhelming because it seems like new platforms are added all the time. In the following section I provide descriptions of some of the more common features of these platforms; an alphabetical list of the more popular platforms that academics and higher education professional should be aware of will also help clarify online opportunities. Although not an exhaustive list, it will serve as a starting point for

TABLE 2.1
Potential Platforms Categorized by Theme

Theme	*Platform*
Book Authorship	About.me Amazon Author Page Goodreads Publisher author page
Citations and Research Networking	Academia.edu Google Scholar Impactstory Institutional website ORCID ResearchGate SSRN
Professional Web Page	About.me LinkedIn Self-hosted professional website Vitae
Social Media	Facebook Google+ Instagram LinkedIn Periscope Pinterest SlideShare Snapchat SoundCloud Twitter
Teaching	Academia.edu MERLOT SlideShare YouTube
Writing and Blogging	Blogger Medium Tumblr WordPress

thinking about all the places you could be represented online (see Table 2.1 for the list of platforms categorized by theme).

Features

In this section, I describe common features to be found on most online platforms. Keep in mind that an online platform wants you to use its tools successfully, so it may also have descriptions of its more advanced features to help you learn the ropes.

Handle.

Most platforms will require you to create a *handle*, or name for use, when in that online space. For some platforms, this name includes an "@" symbol so that people can direct messages to your name (Twitter is a good example). You will want to consider whether you want to use your actual name (if that is available on the platform) or another kind of representative name. Now that you can more easily post across multiple platforms simultaneously (e.g., you can post a picture to Instagram and have it also post to Facebook at the same time), it is helpful if you have the same handle across platforms. This also makes you easier to locate if people know you on one platform but want to find you on another.

Profiles.

Many platforms are based on the idea that you will create a public profile that shares information about you with other users. Each platform has its own privacy guidelines, so you should make sure to read them carefully if you want to share only certain kinds of information publicly (e.g., I do not share my birthday on any platform). Although each profile will look a little different, most include your name, your location, a brief bio statement, and an image to represent you. Depending on the platform, you will also be able to share information about your workplace, your professional experience, and your presentations and publications.

Text-based sharing.

Many platforms such as Twitter, Facebook, and LinkedIn have options for you to write and share "updates" about your life and work. This text-based sharing has different length limitations depending on the platform (e.g., Twitter currently only allows 280 characters), but this kind of sharing is standard across most areas where you might create a presence online (see Box 2.1 for a best practice on sharing links).

Image sharing.

Many platforms now include the option to share pictures and other images, and this has been made especially easy with platform apps available for smartphones. Instagram is one of the more popular image-sharing platforms, but it is also now widely accepted that including images with posts on spaces like Twitter, Facebook, and Medium helps to get more views from people who are scrolling through a long list of updates.

BOX 2.1.
Sharing links.

When sharing links on any platform, consider creating a "short link" through a service like bit.ly or tiny.url. Short links are better for platforms where you have length limitations for posts, but they are also more aesthetically pleasing than the long string of letters and numbers that some web addresses include.

GIFs.
Graphic interchange format software creates short clips of moving images that can be posted on spaces like Twitter and Facebook. They can also be shared via text messaging on some smartphones. Many GIFs are humorous in nature and some also include a short caption at the bottom of the moving image to help explain the image's content.

Video sharing.
Some platforms also include the option of sharing video, such as Facebook, Instagram, Periscope, Snapchat, and YouTube. Given the different audiences for each platform, different video lengths are recommended. For example, a 10-minute video is probably better posted to YouTube than to Facebook, where people are expecting to scroll through lots of updates relatively quickly.

Live video sharing.
There are several platforms that now allow live video sharing, including Facebook, Periscope, Instagram, and others. These platforms allow you to stream a live video that users can watch and respond to in real time. Some platforms (Facebook is one) keep a recording of these videos for people to watch later. These videos are linked through your profile on the platform so that your followers can view them; you can also make your live videos public for all to see.

Platforms

In the following platform descriptions, you will find that several of the examples provided are my own. I do this for the following reasons: (a) I can control these profiles and know that the link will not go away as soon as this book is published, thus making it obsolete, and (b) I want to offer an example of what one academic and higher education professional can look like across various platforms. For those platforms where I have no presence, I have supplied an example of another academic or higher education professional who has been using (and hopefully continues to use) that platform for some time. For your convenience, these and additional examples for all the platforms listed here can be found at the book's companion website at www.mypiobook.com, along with links to each platform. I also welcome you to submit your own examples for inclusion there by e-mailing contact@katielinder.work

About.me.
(https://about.me): Online platform that allows you to create a one-page website where people can find out about you and your work when they search for you online. On this website, you can post an image, a short bio, links to your other social media profiles, as well as a "call to action" link that could allow people to purchase your book, sign up for your newsletter, or a range of other actions.

Example: https://about.me/katielinder

Academia.edu.
(www.academia.edu): Social media site designed for academics to share their work. The profile that users set up is similar to a CV and allows you to share various publications, syllabi, and other artifacts of your academic work. You can follow other users to find out about their latest publications and you can also communicate with other users through the platform to ask questions or to share more about your professional life and work. This platform offers both free and paid features.

Example: https://oregonstate.academia.edu/KatieLinder

Amazon Author Page.
(https://authorcentral.amazon.com): If you have published a book, you can create an Amazon Author Page that includes a profile with information about you and your books. Amazon Author Pages can be "followed" by people who want to hear about your future publications.

Example: http://amazon.com/author/kathrynlinder

Blogger.
(www.blogger.com): Blogging platform where you can create a website and post regular long-form updates about any topic. Blogger allows you to choose a "theme" to customize the look and feel of your blog with different website structures, backgrounds, fonts, and headers.

Example: http://getalifephd.blogspot.com/ or http://phdtalk.blogspot.ca/

Facebook.
(https://facebook.com): Social media site where users post updates using words, images, and video. Facebook includes options for users to have a "profile," a "page," or to create a "group" that other users can join and contribute content to. Facebook can be used more personally, to connect with family and friends, or professionally, to promote a business. Facebook also has the option of streaming video live.

Example: www.facebook.com/DrJosieAhlquist/

Goodreads.
(https://goodreads.com): Platform where you can publicly share what you are currently reading, what you have read in the past, and what you want to read in the future. Recently purchased by Amazon, Goodreads also includes a feature for authors where you can create a special profile to share information about your books, link to a blog, offer periodic updates, or create book giveaways.

Example: www.goodreads.com/author/show/7769629.Kathryn_E_Linder

Google+.
(https://plus.google.com/discover): Social media site where you can create "collections" of text-based updates, images, video, and other digital artifacts for your

followers to see and share. You can also build and join communities on a range of topics or issues.

Example: https://plus.google.com/u/0/+KathrynLinder

Google Scholar.
(https://scholar.google.com): Platform that allows you to publicly share your published work and the citation rates for that work, including an h-index (a common citation metric) that is calculated by Google. Once you sign up for a Google Scholar account, Google will alert you when a new citation should be added to your profile; you can also manually add citations as needed.

Example: http://bit.ly/2rZFBxk

Impactstory.
(https://impactstory.org): Website where you can track the impacts of your research and receive achievement badges based on how much your research is shared on social media sites such as Twitter. Impactstory also has an emphasis on open access, so once you create a profile you can see what percentage of your work is openly available.

Example: https://impactstory.org/u/0000-0002-7486-7665

Instagram.
(www.instagram.com): Social media platform that is image based. Users upload pictures and other images and share them using short captions and hashtags. Depending on who you follow, your Instagram feed may be a mixture of personal updates from friends and family and business posts from larger retailers and small businesses. Instagram also offers a "Stories" feature where users can share short videos that are available for 24 hours. Recently, Instagram also added a feature for users to share live-streamed video via the platform. Although Instagram has a website, the platform is best used through the app available for smartphones.

Example: www.instagram.com/katie_linder/

Institutional website.
If you are affiliated with an institution, you probably have a web page on your institutional site where you can post an image of yourself, your contact information, and a basic bio statement. Some institutional websites also allow you to post a copy of your CV or résumé or have additional features.

Example: https://ecampus.oregonstate.edu/staff/bio/linderk.htm

LinkedIn.
(https://linkedin.com): Social networking site for professionals. Each profile, depending on how detailed you make it, can be equivalent to an online CV or résumé. On LinkedIn, you can connect with other professionals, post updates, create and join

professional groups, and offer recommendations to and receive them from other professionals you have worked with. LinkedIn also has a feature whereby other users can endorse you for particular skills and then includes these endorsements on your public profile.

Example: www.linkedin.com/in/katie-linder-869ba56

Medium.
(https://medium.com): Group blogging platform where you can post long-form essays about any topic, tag those essays, and share them with people who search for content on Medium. You can follow other users and be followed so that people are aware when you have posted something new. Medium also allows you to create a "publication" where you can group similar posts together or copublish content with other authors under the same branded publication name. To comment on, like, or share posts from Medium, you need to create a profile, but you can create a profile without submitting any blog posts yourself.

Example: https://medium.com/@katie__linder

MERLOT.
(www.merlot.org): Open educational resource (OER) repository where you can search for, post, and review educational content that has been made freely available. If you are regularly creating content for your courses (websites, case studies, simulations, etc.) and would like to share those resources, you can create a profile on MERLOT and post information so that people can find and use what you have created. Content is searchable by topic, discipline, and a range of other categories.

Example: http://bit.ly/2hUhluN

ORCID.
(https://orcid.org): Website that allows you to create a persistent digital identifier for your research and data collections. Once you have created an ORCID profile, you can use your ORCID identifier on other websites such as Impactstory to import information about your publications and scholarship. ORCID profiles can be tied to your institutional affiliation as well.

Example: http://orcid.org/0000-0002-7486-7665

Periscope.
(www.periscope.tv): Platform to stream and record live video via a mobile app, with videos also available for viewing on the web. Users can search and follow channels on all kinds of topics and be alerted when new live videos are streaming. Videos can also be recorded for later posting on video aggregation sites like YouTube.

Example: www.periscope.tv/HigherEdScope/

Pinterest.
(https://pinterest.com): Social media site that, similar to Instagram, is image based. Pinterest users can create "boards" of "pinned" pictures and images to group like content in one space. For example, many Pinterest users create vision boards for areas of their home when they are planning a remodel. Recipes are another common area of content frequently pinned on the platform. Boards and images can be shared with others and repinned by other users. Images that are posted on Pinterest typically include short descriptions in the image caption as well as a link to the originator of the picture or image.

Example: www.pinterest.com/katie__linder/

Publisher author page.
If you have published a book, your publisher will often create an author page for you with information about the book, any bonus materials you have created, and how to purchase it.

Example: http://bit.ly/2rVk0XZ

ResearchGate.
(https://researchgate.com): Platform for sharing research. User profiles, similar to Academia.edu, are like a CV or résumé and include detailed information about your work experience, publications, grants received, and other professional accomplishments. You can follow other researchers through the platform, as well as have people follow you. By curating who you follow on ResearchGate, you can be updated about the latest published work in your field or discipline.

Example: www.researchgate.net/profile/Kathryn_Linder

Self-hosted professional website.
You may choose to create your own professional website where you can share information about your work experience, publications, presentations, or other artifacts of your professional life. A self-hosted professional website will offer you the most autonomy in terms of website design and control of content. (This topic is also covered in more detail in chapter 7.)

Example: https://katielinder.work

SlideShare.
(www.slideshare.net): Platform where users can upload and share PowerPoint presentations and other documents in a public or private forum. SlideShares can be embedded on a website or shared via several social media platforms. This platform was recently acquired by LinkedIn.

Example: www.slideshare.net/ericstoller

Snapchat.
(www.snapchat.com): App-based platform where users can post and send images and short videos that will self-destruct after a matter of seconds. Images can also be augmented with drawings, filters, and text.

Example: No examples can be offered for Snapchat because of the brevity of content availability, but common uses for Snapchat include "day-in-the-life" posts where users share image and video updates from throughout their day (this is also a common use of Instagram Stories).

Social Science Research Network (SSRN).
(www.ssrn.com): Research sharing platform where scholars can disseminate web-based versions of their work via a range of research networks broken down by field and discipline. Users can search for research by title, abstract, keywords, and authors. Whereas some research posted to SSRN is peer reviewed, other content includes documents such as conference papers, thought pieces, course materials, and white papers. The site ranks top authors, papers, and organizations based on download and citation rates.

Example: http://bit.ly/2iplojT

SoundCloud.
(www.soundcloud.com): Social media site for sharing and listening to audio files. Users can post audio files, listen to podcasts and music, and leave comments on other people's uploads. SoundCloud also allows for audio upload via RSS feed and can be connected to audio management platforms for easy sharing of regular audio productions like podcasts.

Example: https://soundcloud.com/ygt_podcast

Tumblr.
(www.tumblr.com): Blogging platform where users can post a range of content including text, images, videos, quotes, links, and more. Users can follow each other's blogs and repost content from the blogs they follow.

Example: http://wheninacademia.tumblr.com/ or http://academicssay.tumblr.com/

Twitter.
(https://twitter.com): *Microblogging* platform where users post updates of 280 characters or less. Twitter uses hashtags to organize topics and conversations. The use of hashtags also allows for "tweet chats," which are conversations that happen in real time and that can be followed publicly.

Example: https://twitter.com/Katie__Linder

Vitae.
(https://chroniclevitae.com): Platform created by *The Chronicle of Higher Education* as an "online career hub" for academics and higher education professionals. Users can create a profile, post to community message boards, apply for jobs, or find a mentor.

Example: https://chroniclevitae.com/people/49605-dr-katie-linder/profile

WordPress.
(https://wordpress.org): Web hosting, content management, and blogging platform where users can create websites and blogs to share content on any topic. WordPress is well known for its range of "themes" that users can choose and apply to their blogs and websites to create sites that are customized to their aesthetic preferences.

Example: https://patthomson.net/ or https://explorationsofstyle.com/

YouTube.
(https://youtube.com): Video hosting platform where users can create their own video channels to upload and share video content. Users can also subscribe to other video channels, create and share playlists of videos, and review video content. YouTube has also become a space for instructors to upload lecture and other course content for viewing by students, or to find supplemental course materials that have been created and posted by others. Some researchers are also now using YouTube to share about their scholarship (see Box 2.2 for an academic YouTuber).

Example: www.youtube.com/c/KathrynLinder

Learning New Platforms

Many times we may not join an online platform because the learning curve for that platform seems too high. For example, I got easily overwhelmed when I reengaged with Facebook after five years away as part of my research for this book. It took me months to figure out the differences among profiles, pages, groups, and the possible uses of Facebook for my personal and professional life. As another example, I also waited quite some time before diving into Instagram Stories, a live video feature similar to Snapchat where your recordings disappear after a limited time. To give you a sense of my thought process, I needed to answer certain questions before I felt I could get started with the Stories feature:

- How much room on my phone will videos take up once I start recording them?
- How frequently should I be posting videos once I start?
- What kinds of content should I include in my Instagram Stories?
- Is it worth my time to post Instagram Stories?
- What are the potential benefits of using this feature?
- Are there any drawbacks to using this feature?

BOX 2.2.
Being a YouTuber as a higher education professional.

Sara Langworthy
Speaker, consultant, author, and YouTuber

Find Sara online:
Professional website: www.drlangworthy.com
Twitter: https://twitter.com/drlangworthy
LinkedIn: www.linkedin.com/in/drlangworthy/
YouTube: http://bit.ly/2qIC4nZ

After receiving her PhD in developmental psychology in 2011, Sara knew that she did not want to pursue a traditional academic research position. She was committed to nurturing excitement, playfulness, and energy in her professional life, and that did not seem to mesh with the typical academic roles that were available to her.

As Sara thought about different avenues for her work, a consistent theme was the importance of getting information into the hands of people who needed it. Sara began to explore science communication and how to balance sharing accurate scientific information while also providing entertainment value—not always an easy task.

Sara's passion for science communication led her to start a YouTube channel called *Developmental Enthusiast*, where her videos now receive tens of thousands of views. Through these videos, Sara shares her enthusiasm for learning and science. This creative outlet also allows Sara to make meaningful connections with her audience, provide valuable information, and create usable content that can be easily shared to help her promote her small business.

By combining her creativity and expertise, Sara has developed a memorable online presence for herself that nicely augments other areas of her digital life.

Admittedly, rather than seek answers to these questions, I procrastinated from using the feature. It was a lot easier to just ignore it than try to muddle my way through figuring it out. The turning point for me was when my publisher asked me to consider doing more live video. The person in charge of promotions with Stylus had been attending social media conferences that were pushing live video as the Next Big Thing, so I agreed to look into it.

Tips for Engaging With a New Platform

There are several steps that I can recommend if you are trying to decide how best to engage with a new platform or platform feature.

Watch how other people use it.
Many of the people I followed on Instagram were using the Stories feature and some of them were clearly power users who were posting videos several times a day. By

watching their videos, I started to notice what I liked and what I did not. I also realized that I almost never turned on sound for the videos as I watched them, so videos that used the text feature with words and images combined were more effective for me. Also, many of the videos that had text included had a painted color behind the text that made it easier to read. Last, I noticed a range of "stickers," filters, and silly overlays that people used in their videos and decided that I could ignore those for the most part. As I watched, I filed all this information away.

Do some research.
For my question about the file space on my phone for video creation, it was pretty easy to do some Google searching to find the answer. It was also easy to find some step-by-step tutorials of best practices for the Stories feature once it had been out for quite some time. If you do not care about being on the bleeding edge of new feature releases, just wait for a walk-through blog post by a power user to pick up some tips for your own use.

Explore the feature.
After weeks of watching other people's Stories and doing some preliminary blog research, I found something I wanted to take a short video of, and I experimented with length, text features, and colored paint options. I deleted some of the videos I recorded and kept others. I also focused mostly on the elements of the Stories feature that I had liked the most in other videos I was drawn to.

Dive in when you are ready.
Finally, I posted the video in my Stories so that I could view it in the platform and see what other people would see. I also kept an eye on my post for the next 24 hours or so (until it disappeared) to see what kind of metrics I would be able to collect about who and how many people watched the video. Once I made one video, I made a couple more so that I could see how the videos worked when they were strung together.

Getting started with this new feature was a lot easier than I had originally thought. In part, this is because social media platforms want to make your engagement with their features as simple as possible. They want their users to engage with all the features of their platforms. A simple takeaway is that we often make joining new platforms or launching new features seem more difficult than it really is. Remember that sometimes you will only find the right platforms and features for you through experimentation (see Box 2.3 for one example of a higher education professional who used this method to find the right online spaces for her).

To get started with these new-to-you platforms, I recommend the following:

- *Explore the platform's website.* To get a sense of the goal of the platform, its features, and the general audience that it is aimed toward, visit the platform's website and support pages. (All of the platforms listed in this chapter have

BOX 2.3.
Experimenting to find the right online spaces.

Laura Gogia
Principal, Bandwidth Strategies

Find Laura online:
Professional website: http://lauragogia.com
Blog: https://googleguacamole.wordpress.com
Twitter: https://twitter.com/GoogleGuacamole
LinkedIn: www.linkedin.com/in/laura-gogia-29019067/

Laura began engaging online when she struggled to find a personal and professional development network face-to-face. From the time that she was in graduate school to her current work in leadership development, she has connected with other people online to learn from them. For Laura, the world is her office as she nurtures digital connections to expand her "local" scholarly networks.

Importantly, however, Laura's online presence has matured over time. In the beginning of her experimentations online, Laura would mimic the digital presence of others. After a period of "teenage years" where she worked to find herself by experimenting with different platforms, Laura has seen both her use of platforms and her digital relationships grow and change.

Through questioning why her digital peers make the choices they do, through experimentation, and through her own reflections on what it means for her to be a professional online, Laura has developed more confidence in her online presence.

Laura now uses different platforms for different purposes. She feels more secure in her voice and more proactive about reaching out to others. Laura's comfort online is palpable and she now has an online presence that others try to emulate.

websites included in the glossary at the end of this book and are hyperlinked on the book's companion website.)

- *Read reviews.* Seek out reviews of the platform, preferably by academics if you can find them. User reviews are a great way to find out if a new platform is worth your time, especially if you are comparing one platform to another.
- *Find someone who is already using the platform.* Talking with current platform users about their experiences is a good way to learn the pros and cons of a new platform. In particular, you will want to know what they are gaining from being a member of that platform, how much time they are taking to maintain their presence on that platform and engage with other users, and their honest opinion of the quality of the platform and whether they recommend it to others.

Once you have done each of these things, you will have a better sense of the goals of each platform and whether that platform might be a good fit for you. Remember that if you are still not sure about a platform after completing the steps outlined in this chapter, consider a trial period on the platform. Decide on an amount of time for registering, setting up your profile, and using the platform in which you can decide whether you want to continue.

As you can see from the range of options presented in this chapter, academics and higher education professionals have a lot of choices as to where and how to be online. In the following two chapters, you will have the opportunity to further explore where you are now and where you want to be in the future.

EVALUATING YOUR CURRENT DIGITAL IDENTITY

Getting Started

Each of the six components described in chapter 1 has a different application to each area of your online identity. You may also feel that some of the criteria should be prioritized over others given the current state of your online presence. Review the following list (returning to chapter 1 for a quick overview of each term if needed) and rank each of the criteria based on what you think might need the most work based on your professional stage and career goals:

_____ Consistency
_____ Professionalism
_____ Accuracy
_____ Organization
_____ Quality
_____ Representativeness

As you begin to self-evaluate your current digital identity, it is important to find all the places that you are online. Table 3.1 offers a comprehensive (but not exhaustive) list of places where you might already be present online (if any of the platforms are unfamiliar to you, they are each described in more detail in the previous chapter). Take a moment to run through the list, checking the appropriate box for each platform. A few blank rows have also been included for additional platforms where you may have profiles but are not included on this list.

Once you have gone through the list of platforms in Table 3.1, divide the list into two categories based on whether or not you are currently on the platform. Enter each platform into Table 3.2.

Using Table 3.2, start with the category of platforms where you are currently already present online. This is the main category that you will be exploring in this chapter. To begin, go through each of the platforms and ask yourself the following basic questions:

TABLE 3.1
Potential Platforms and Level of Engagement

Platform	Currently on This Platform	Currently Not on This Platform, but Have Heard of It	Have Never Heard of This Platform
About.me			
Academia.edu			
Amazon Author Page			
Any blogging platform			
Facebook			
Goodreads			
Google+			
Google Scholar			
Impactstory			
Instagram			
Institutional website			
LinkedIn			
MERLOT			
ORCID			
Periscope			
Pinterest			
Publisher author page			
ResearchGate			
Self-hosted professional website			
SlideShare			
Snapchat			
SoundCloud			
SSRN			
Twitter			
Vitae			
YouTube			

TABLE 3.2
Platform Use Organized by Level of Engagement

Currently on This Platform	*Currently Not on This Platform*

- Do I know the username and password for this platform (i.e., do I know how to sign in)?

- When was the last time I visited this platform?

- Is my profile on this platform being maintained or is it dormant (i.e., not kept up-to-date)?

- Is there anything about this platform that is confusing to me?

- Do I care about this platform?

- Has my engagement in this platform brought value to my professional life? My personal life?

- Is this a platform that I want to continue to maintain in the future?

For example, if I was asking these questions about my own engagement on Twitter, I might say the following:

- Do I know the username and password for this platform (i.e., do I know how to sign in)?
  - *Yes, I have the username and password stored for all Twitter accounts that I manage.*
- When was the last time I visited this platform?
  - *I last visited this platform earlier today.*
- Is my profile on this platform being maintained or is it dormant (i.e., not kept up-to-date)?
  - *Yes, my profile is up-to-date with correct links, a recent headshot, and accurate information in my bio statement.*
- Is there anything about this platform that is confusing to me?
  - *Not really. Once I figured out hashtags and image-sizing requirements I felt pretty comfortable using the platform.*
- Do I care about this platform?
  - *Yes. This is an important platform for promoting my work and connecting with other scholars.*
- Has my engagement in this platform brought value to my professional life? My personal life?
  - *Yes. I have met several new people and connected with them in person at conferences and I have been offered professional opportunities directly related to relationships I have built on Twitter.*
- Is this a platform that I want to continue to maintain in the future?
  - *Yes.*

However, asking these questions about my engagement on Google+ shows a different set of answers:

- Do I know the username and password for this platform (i.e., do I know how to sign in)?
  - *Yes, but only because it's part of my larger Google account where I access Gmail.*
- When was the last time I visited this platform?
  - *Maybe at some point within the last six months? I'm not really sure.*
- Is my profile on this platform being maintained or is it dormant (i.e., not kept up-to-date)?
  - *I updated my profile here over the summer with my digital refresh, but I don't actively engage on this platform, so I would say it's dormant.*
- Is there anything about this platform that is confusing to me?
  - *Yes. In fact, I'm not really sure I know how the platform works, all of its features, or how it's connected to other areas of Google, like my Gmail or Google Hangouts. I think the "Circles" feature is part of Google+, but I'm not sure about that either.*
- Do I care about this platform?

- *Not really. I don't think that many academics are using Google+ and I don't really see any benefits of the features of that platform that I don't get on other platforms I utilize more regularly.*
- Has my engagement in this platform brought value to my professional life? My personal life?
  - *No. I haven't really connected with anyone on Google+ professionally or personally and I don't follow anyone there who posts regularly.*
- Is this a platform that I want to continue to maintain in the future?
  - *Yes, but only because it's one I cannot delete. Maybe this is a platform that I need to spend some time learning more about to make sure I'm not missing any opportunities I'm just not aware of.*

By asking yourself these questions, you will learn where you are most active online, what profiles and platforms you visit the most, and what platforms or profiles you may want to retire (i.e., delete) because you are no longer updating and maintaining them. These questions will also allow you to see what areas of particular platforms you may need to learn more about to become more comfortable using that platform. In answering the previous questions, you may also decide that you want to revive some dormant platforms or refresh some that need updating.

Self-Evaluating Your Current Online Presence

Once you have answered this first set of questions, you will want to set aside some time to go through each platform where you already have an online presence and evaluate your profile and engagement using the categories discussed in chapter 1. Using the guiding questions in the rubric offered in Table 3.3, explore each platform where you have profiles to self-assess levels of consistency, professionalism, accuracy, organization, quality, and representativeness. You will see that each of the six criteria has been matched with the four areas of your online presence. Guiding questions are offered in each part of the rubric to help in self-assessment. Some of the questions will be applicable to individual online platforms, whereas others will need to be applied across the online platforms as a whole. Use Table 3.4 to make notes about each platform, paying attention to where you have strengths and where you need to make changes.

After you have visited each platform, ask yourself the following:

- Where am I most comfortable?
- Which is the strongest and where can I send people to first learn about my work and professional accomplishments?
- What platform needs the most work or refreshing?

While completing this exercise, I recommend noting changes for the future rather than making changes as you go. Chapter 5 will offer additional concrete tips for making sure that your notes do not go to waste.

TABLE 3.3

Applying the Six Criteria to Your Online Identity Components

Criterion	Headshot	Bio	Personal Brand	Content
Consistency	Is your headshot consistent across multiple online platforms?	Is your bio statement, even when different lengths, consistent across multiple online platforms?	Is how you choose to portray yourself consistent across multiple online platforms?	Is the content you provide about your professional life consistent across multiple online platforms?
Professionalism	Is your headshot one that you can use across professional contexts?	Does your bio statement focus primarily on your professional accomplishments?	Is the reputation that you are building through your online identities aligned across platforms?	Does the content that you have included adequately represent your professional accomplishments?
Accuracy	Is your headshot up-to-date and representative of how you currently look?	Does your bio statement include an up-to-date and honest portrayal of your professional identity?	Is how you choose to portray your professional accomplishments, networks, and positions up-to-date, accurate, and truthful to the best of your knowledge?	Is the content that you have provided up-to-date, truthful, and representative of your most recent professional accomplishments?
Organization	Is your appearance in your headshot neat and tidy?	Does your bio statement include information in an order that represents how you prioritize your professional identity?	Is how you choose to portray your professional identity offered in a compelling, thoughtful, and intentional way?	Have you intentionally and purposefully organized your content to best represent your professional accomplishments?
Quality	Is your headshot professionally produced?	Is your bio statement a well-thought-out representation of your professional identity?	Does how you choose to portray yourself online demonstrate your commitment to excellence and professionalism?	Is the content that you have provided representative of the best you have to offer of your professional work?
Representativeness	Is your headshot representative of how you want to be viewed as a professional?	When combined, do all your bio statements represent the foundational components of your professional identity? Is anything missing?	Is how you choose to portray yourself online representative of you as a professional?	Does the content that you have included across your online platforms completely represent your professional accomplishments?

TABLE 3.4
Strengths of and Changes Needed for Online Profiles

Platform	Areas of Strength	Things to Change

Once you have completed your review of the places where you already exist online, you will want to turn your attention to the column of Table 3.2 that includes the platforms with which you are not currently actively engaged. Ask yourself the following:

- Are there any specific reasons why I have chosen not to join this platform?
- When was the last time I reviewed this platform to decide if it would be helpful to my professional life?
- How widely used is this platform among people in my professional and personal networks?
- Are there any new features of this platform that have been added since my last encounter that I need to review?

If it is helpful, you can also return to the "Learning New Platforms" section of chapter 2 if you decide you want to add to your current online presence. See Box 3.1 for an example of an academic who regularly reviews his use of online platforms and takes digital sabbaticals.

Engaging on Multiple Platforms

This chapter has offered three layers of review for the platforms where you already exist, those that you are aware of but not actively engaged with, and those you have not yet heard about. Now that you have completed a comprehensive review of your online presence and seen the range of options for where you can be online, you will want to decide where you want to be present online and which platforms you want to prioritize. In the following chapter, you will explore the range of ways that you can represent yourself online, including naming conventions, images, bio statements, and other forms of individual brand management.

Because every platform has its own purpose, and may draw different audiences than other platforms, it is possible that you will be engaging on multiple platforms simultaneously. Indeed, you probably already are if you are like most of the adults discussed in the statistics from the introductory chapter. The following chapter will help you decide where you want to put your energy and how much time you plan to spend on your online presence. To help you get started, consider the following:

- What online platforms make the most sense for me to engage in at this stage in your career?
- Do I want to post the same information across different online profiles, or do I plan to share different content for different platforms and audiences?
- Are there platforms that I plan to engage in solely for personal connections?
- Are there platforms that I plan to engage in solely for professional connections?

BOX 3.1.
Taking a digital sabbatical.

George Veletsianos
Canada research chair and associate professor
Royal Roads University

Find George online:
Professional website: www.veletsianos.com
Twitter: https://twitter.com/veletsianos
YouTube: http://bit.ly/2qClqrA

George researches and writes about the digital lives of students and faculty. In 2016, he published *Social Media in Academia: Networked Scholars* (Veletsianos, 2016a). Given this professional interest, George is heavily active online across a range of social media platforms. For George, being online helps him to understand digital involvement, to make sense of how faculty participate online, and to explore why faculty are and are not online.

Although it is true that you can find George in most of the usual places, including Twitter and YouTube, it might surprise you to know how seriously George takes the idea of a digital sabbatical. Once a week, George completely unplugs from the online world, steps away from his screens, and takes a 24-hour break.

At first, he worried that being unplugged might be difficult, but so far there have been only positive benefits. George also regularly reviews his online presence. In the past, he has removed himself from platforms like Facebook to focus his online energies elsewhere.

As an expert in academics' engagement on social media, George takes intentional steps in his own online presence to make sure each platform is helping, rather than hurting, his work and life.

- How frequently will I revisit the platforms I have chosen for self-assessment of my profiles and do I want to continue on those platforms?

Each of these questions should offer you a better sense of how you plan to engage across multiple online platforms.

4

CHOOSING HOW TO REPRESENT YOURSELF ONLINE

Professional Branding

Although the term *brand* can be a turnoff for many academics, the concept is becoming more and more important as the idea of online professional presence has become increasingly solidified. While some consider the idea of individual branding to be too commercial, too much like selling out, or too narcissistic, it is also true that the person you are online (and in real life, for that matter) needs to be differentiated from the other people around you. In many niche areas of academia, and certainly at your institution, you may be the only person who can conduct the research that you do or who can teach the classes that you do. Based on your disciplinary and other training, you already have a professional brand that separates you from many of your colleagues. Once you add in your unique personality and other professional strengths, it becomes easier to identify how you might want to more intentionally use your unique brand identity in online spaces.

Another term for personal branding that is more commonly used in academia is *expertise*. As academics and higher education professionals establish themselves as experts in particular fields or areas, they become known in particular ways. For example, an academic may become known as an excellent grant writer; a generous collaborator; or, on a less positive note, a grumpy department chair. In whatever ways that you choose to engage online, you have the option to decide and curate the kinds of information you share about your professional life and to craft a form of expertise, or a brand, for yourself. The most important part of representing your brand online is keeping in mind that who you are online is the person whom you have chosen to be. A lot of what makes up your brand is entirely within your control.

Using the following guiding questions, make note of the elements that might be part of your professional brand:

- When people talk about me when I am not present, what kinds of things do I want them to say?

- What do I want to be known for regionally, nationally, or internationally?

- What kinds of professional values are most important for me to demonstrate on a consistent basis?

- What do my colleagues think I do phenomenally well?

- If I had to be known as an expert in just one area, what would it be?

- What is my favorite thing to teach others about?

Choosing How to Be Online

Based on the range of platforms outlined in chapter 2, you can see that how you choose to be online is related to several fundamental factors. The first factor is what you are hoping to accomplish by being online. For example, are you hoping to promote your work to a broader audience, connect with colleagues, establish yourself as an expert in a particular field or topic area, or find additional resources or support for your professional work? Each of these goals might lead you to different platforms. For example, the categories offered in Table 2.1 in chapter 2 offer some examples of the range of ways that an academic or higher education professional can engage online: as a book author or researcher, through networking and collaborating with colleagues, by sharing ideas and resources, via connecting with students, or as a producer of writing or other creative scholarly works.

Before signing up for any new platform, take a moment to write down your general goals for the online platforms that you want to join (keeping in mind that these goals might also change over time):

Goal #1: _____

Goal #2: _____

Goal #3: _____

The second factor in choosing how to be online is deciding what parts of your identity you want to share with others in an online space. In my case, I want to share work that I produce (e.g., books, essays, and podcasts), connect with other researchers (for both current and future collaborations), and make sure that I know about the latest developments in my field. When deciding what you want to share, it is also important to think about the current stage of your career. If you are just starting out, it may be important for you to build a strong network of colleagues in your field from a range of institutions. Or, if you are in a pre- or nontenure position, you may want to take extra cautions about what and how you share online. On the other hand, if you are a midcareer or senior scholar, it may be that you already feel you are well networked and being online is more about promoting your work to a younger generation of scholars. You also want to consider how much personal information to include in your online presence (see Box 4.1 for one higher education professional's decision-making process regarding sharing personal information).

When building your online presence, it is important to look at your identity from a holistic perspective so that you can be as broadly representative of yourself as you choose. For example, my online identity includes a range of roles such as researcher, writer, author, public speaker, and podcaster. Take a moment to write down all the words and phrases that you might use to describe the identities that you will want to include in your online presence (a sample list is included in Box 4.2 if you need help getting started):

_____   _____   _____

_____   _____   _____

_____   _____   _____

_____   _____   _____

_____   _____   _____

_____   _____   _____

_____   _____   _____

_____   _____   _____

_____   _____   _____

BOX 4.1.
Getting personal online.

Josh Eyler
Director, Center for Teaching Excellence
Adjunct associate professor of humanities
Rice University

Find Josh online:
Professional website: https://josheyler.wordpress.com
Twitter: https://twitter.com/joshua_r_eyler
LinkedIn: www.linkedin.com/in/joshua-eyler-88583338/

For most of his academic career, Josh chose to keep his personal and professional online lives separate. He used Twitter to communicate with professional colleagues and Facebook for family and friends. That all changed when his wife faced a serious health issue and Josh needed to use his entire network to bring attention to her situation. He chose to blur his personal and professional boundaries in ways that he never had before.

Josh used Twitter and the hashtag #forKariann to direct messages to his insurance company and share his wife's situation with his broader network. This resulted in a social media campaign that drew support from friends, colleagues, and strangers. The unexpectedly strong response, with hundreds of uses of the hashtag and frequent retweets and reposts, also attracted local news coverage and national media attention in higher education publications.

Through this experience, Josh realized the power of social media networks to personalize professional relationships. He found that by blurring the lines between his personal and professional lives, he deepened and enriched his relationships with academic community members in online environments.

Even better, following the social media campaign, Josh's wife was approved for a rare treatment that had been twice denied.

A third factor to consider when choosing how to be online is how long and how frequently you want to engage with your online platforms. Some platforms can lie relatively dormant and require infrequent updates whereas other platforms will demand that you engage daily (or multiple times per day) to get all the benefits of that platform. (Figure 4.1 offers an overview of an engagement spectrum for some of the platforms discussed previously.) An important thing to keep in mind is that your engagement online will probably be more time-consuming in the beginning when you are just learning a new platform. It is likely that your time investment will decrease as the platform becomes more familiar to you. Chapters 5 and 8 include more information about maintaining your online profiles and choosing what to post and share on each one.

BOX 4.2.

Sample list of identity words and phrases.

Academic	Creator	Principal Investigator
Adjunct	Designer	Presenter
Administrator	Developer	Professor
Adviser	Facilitator	Researcher
Artist	Freelancer	Scholar
Author	Grant Writer	Scientist
Coach	Instructor	Speaker
Collaborator	Maker	Specialist
Consultant	PhD Candidate	Teacher
Coordinator	Podcaster	Writer

Figure 4.1. An engagement spectrum for online platforms.

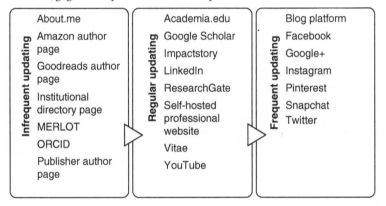

Take a moment to think about how much time you already spend engaging with online platforms. Consider how much time you spend watching YouTube, participating in social media, and updating various profiles that you might already have. What are the most frequent times of day when you are online? For example, do you mostly go online in the morning, at lunchtime, or after work? Or do you mostly engage online during the weekends? If you are not sure, use the time tracker in Table 4.1 to log your online engagement over the course of a week. You may find that you are spending more time online than you thought.

Once you have a sense of your current online engagement and you have considered what you hope to gain from your online presence, decide how much time you think is reasonable for you to spend each day engaging online. Note that the amount of time that you choose to engage online or your level of engagement with a particular platform may change during certain periods of your professional career. For example, you may spend more time on LinkedIn when actively job searching or more time on your Amazon author platform when promoting a new book. The following

TABLE 4.1
Time Tracker Tool to Measure Your Online Engagement

Time	Monday	Tuesday	Wednesday	Thursday	Friday	Saturday	Sunday
1 a.m.							
2 a.m.							
3 a.m.							
4 a.m.							
5 a.m.							
6 a.m.							
7 a.m.							
8 a.m.							
9 a.m.							
10 a.m.							
11 a.m.							
12 p.m.							
1 p.m.							
2 p.m.							
3 p.m.							
4 p.m.							
5 p.m.							
6 p.m.							
7 p.m.							
8 p.m.							
9 p.m.							
10 p.m.							
11 p.m.							
12 a.m.							

guiding questions can help you to think about what might be coming up for you that would require more engagement on one platform than another:

- Am I currently on the market, or do I plan to go on the market in the next year?
- Am I currently working on a book, or have I recently published a book?
- Am I actively producing scholarly articles, reports, or other research outputs?
- Do I want to increase the number of people in my professional social network?

TABLE 4.2
Upcoming Engagements That Necessitate Increased Online Presence

January	February	March	April
May	June	July	August
September	October	November	December

TABLE 4.3
Examples of Upcoming Engagements That Necessitate Increased Online Presence

January	February	March	April
			Launched podcast #1
May	**June**	**July**	**August**
		Launched podcast #2	Speaking event
September	**October**	**November**	**December**
Webinar re: national study research	Research report released	Book published	

- Do I have an upcoming sabbatical?
- Do I engage in any consulting or service provision that requires self-promotion?
- Do I have artifacts from teaching, research, or my professional service obligations that deserve to be shared with a broader audience?

Table 4.2 offers a calendar to help you think through the upcoming year and whether you expect any major occurrences that might necessitate increases in your online presence and engagement.

Table 4.3 offers an example of a filled-in table based on my projects list from 2016. As you can see from Table 4.3, half of the months included the need to promote something, whether a report release, a webinar about research results, a new podcast show, or another form of publication such as a book that came out in November.

Many projects take months of preparation, so think ahead as you fill in the calendar offered in Table 4.2. What is coming up for you in the next year that might require more online engagement? Alternatively, filling out Table 4.2 might demonstrate that you have a quiet year coming up or that you have more personal accomplishments (e.g., having a new baby, taking a long trip, or getting married) that will take precedence over your professional goals. Whatever you discover through this reflection, use it to help you decide where and how much you want to be online. (See Box 4.3 for one higher education professional's take on what being consistent across online platforms means for her and her business.)

BOX 4.3.
Being consistent online.

Meggin McIntosh
Higher education consultant

Find Meggin online:
Professional website: https://meggin.com
Twitter: https://twitter.com/megginmcintosh
LinkedIn: www.linkedin.com/in/MegginMcIntosh
YouTube: www.youtube.com/user/MegginMcIntosh

With Meggin, what you see is what you get, whether you meet her face-to-face or online. Her choices about her online presence are all founded in a philosophy of authenticity. If you follow her online, you will learn about her business and services, but you will also know who she is voting for in an upcoming election.

Meggin has intentionally chosen to share humor and real-life stories across all of her platforms. She sets boundaries for her online presence in the same way that she does for her offline life—if she would not say something to you face-to-face, she also will not say it online. This results in a consistency across all of her online platforms and with her day-to-day life.

These choices about how to be online have allowed Meggin to walk the talk that she also advocates for her clients. Because Meggin's mission is to inspire joyful work, she uses her online engagement to connect authentically with people who have similar goals. Her passion is to help people to live their right lives, so she purposefully shares what matters to her and why.

For Meggin, someone who does not like what she is sharing online or who she is probably would not be a good match for her business. With over seven billion people in the world, Meggin knows she can still be successful even if not everyone likes her style and message. She can be her authentic self everywhere—online and offline.

Choosing a Name for Your Profiles

As you create your profiles online, you will need to create handles or names for your pages. The following sections delineate some best practices to keep in mind.

Be recognizable across platforms.

If you use the same name for each profile, it makes it easier for people to find you. This was one reason why I recently rebranded online to be "Katie" instead of "Kathryn"—because I use the name Katie 95% of the time, that was the name people searched for when trying to find me online.

Check name availability across platforms.

Before you make a final decision about the handle that you plan to use for one platform, check its availability on the other main platforms you plan to use; it is possible that your name of choice will be available on one but not all. If you plan to be active on several platforms, it is helpful when your name is the same because it can be easier for others to tag you and to find you.

Create a memorable name.

The most memorable name that you can choose is your actual name, but if that is not available, try to create something as close to it as possible. For example, on Instagram, Katie_Linder was available, but it was not available on Twitter. If you find me on Twitter, you will see that I have the same convention, but I have used *two* underscores within my name. I would recommend not using numbers in your name (i.e., Joan458), because it makes it harder for people to search and find you. It is better, when possible, to include both your first and last name in the handle so that if people search your name, it will come up in the results. Here are some examples of various names that could work if your first choice is taken:

- First_Last
- theactualfirstlast
- realfirstlast
- firstlast_
- last_first

Choosing a Representative Image

When you are creating your online profiles, you will want to make sure to include an image in each one. This makes it easier for people to know they have found the right person, especially if there are several other people with your name. To help as you choose your profile images, the following sections address some best practices to keep in mind.

Choose an image that looks like you.

This may seem obvious, but there are many profile images that are outdated or show the person with a drastically different haircut or facial hair than is currently the case.

Make sure that the picture you choose is similar to how you currently look, and if you make a drastic change take a new picture and update your profiles.

Choose the right size and scale image.
Different platforms will share your profile image in different ways. For example, some offer a rectangle, others a square box, and others a circle. Make sure that the image you choose fits across profiles; this usually means having an image of yourself that is centered. Many platforms also offer an image-cropping feature so you can adjust your image once it is uploaded.

Also, keep in mind that if you choose an image that is the scale of your whole body, it may be hard for someone to recognize you when the image is a small thumbnail size onscreen. Posting a headshot, or an image of you from the shoulders up, ensures that visitors to your profile can clearly see your face.

Choose a quality image.
If you have a blurry image, or an image that is the wrong resolution, it may not render well on all profiles. Try to choose a higher resolution image so that the quality of the image is not compromised when it is posted to a range of platforms that require different file sizes. There are also several user-friendly apps such as Camera+ that can improve image quality.

Crafting an Effective Bio Statement

One of the first things that people will look for when they find you online is your bio statement. This part of your online profile serves a range of purposes:

- It helps people to know whether they want to "follow" you.
- It provides information about your professional context and relationships (who do you work for, what field of study are you in, etc.).
- It offers a glimpse into the things that are most important to you.
- It promotes work or projects that are important to you.

Take a few minutes to peruse an online site where you have a profile. How are people describing themselves? Can you tell the goal of someone's online presence based on the bio statement? You may find that some bio statements are more helpful than others. Some will provide the information you are looking for, whereas others will only offer a name or, in some cases, just a handle that leaves you unsure about who the person actually is in real life.

Using the words and phrases you identified earlier in the chapter, as well as your answers to the guiding questions related to your professional brand, brainstorm some potential taglines that you might be able to use for your online bio statements. Taglines are especially useful on platforms like Twitter where your bio statement is required to be shorter. Although a tagline is nice to have, it can be challenging to write and will require some wordsmithing to make sure that you are fitting in the

BOX 4.4.
An additional resource for crafting taglines.

Hogshead (2014) refers to taglines as "anthems" (pp. 363–388) and devotes an entire chapter to crafting them in her book *How the World Sees You*, so check out that resource if you need additional inspiration.

most important descriptors or pieces of information you want to share. If you have a professional website or an institutional web page that provides more information about you, you can also link to that source of information in your bio or within the profile so that people interested in learning more about you know where to go.

The following sections provide some templates to get you started drafting an effective tagline (see Box 4.4 for an additional resource).

Template #1. Professional and Personal
[Position Title] at [Organization Name] | [Identity Category] | [Identity Category] | Love [enter passions here].

> Example: Researcher at Utah State University | Mother | Auntie | Love exploring the intricacies of global warming and listening to audiobooks

Template #2. Professional and Personal
[Descriptor] | [Descriptor] | [Descriptor] | [Descriptor] | [Descriptor] | [Descriptor]

> Example: Scholar | Teacher | Museum docent | Local theater enthusiast | Reader of all things | Cheese snob

Template #3. Professional and Connection Oriented
[Position Title] at [Organization Name] | Follow me for posts about [Topic Areas of Interest].

> Example: Instructional designer at Purdue University | Follow me for posts about tech, innovation, and productivity hacks

Template #4. Professional and Self-Promotion Oriented
[Position Title] at [Organization Name] and [Descriptor] for [Project Title] | Find me [Action] at [Web Address]

> Example: Executive director of admissions at Georgia State University and creator of #admitme | Find me writing at Medium.com

In the following chapter, you will explore some of the strategies and tools that can help you regularly revise and maintain your online presence across multiple platforms.

5

TOOLS FOR UPDATING AND MANAGING YOUR ONLINE PRESENCE

Getting Started and Sticking With It

Whether you are just starting out with creating new digital profiles or you are work-ing on refreshing old profiles that need an update, building your online presence can feel a bit overwhelming. This chapter is all about helping you find the organizational strategies, accountability structures, and motivation that you need to start your digi-tal updates and to see them through to the end. The last thing you want is to get partway through making changes to your digital profiles, get tired and frustrated, and quit when you are only halfway done. By using the tools in this chapter, you can create a system for making the changes that you need now, as well as a system for managing and maintaining your profiles once you have them up and running.

Organization

As you get started with renovating your digital profiles, one of the most important things you can do is to have a sense of the job that you have in front of you. Go back to the list of profiles that already exist for you in chapter 3 and list out all of the places that you need to visit to look over your profile page and make revisions. Next, create a master list of all tasks you need to do for each platform (note that some will require more work than others). See Table 5.1 for a sample master list. You can also use the six-criterion rubric in chapter 3 to get started with generating tasks that you need to complete for each profile. At a minimum, for each profile you will want to update your profile information, bio statement, and headshot to be accurate and up-to-date; find colleagues and friends to connect with on the platform; and adjust your privacy settings.

As you see from the sample list in Table 5.1, you will need to complete some of the same tasks on each platform, but it can be helpful if your master list of tasks includes each of the items under each platform that you plan to update. It is more likely that you will go platform by platform rather than batch similar tasks, so you

TABLE 5.1
Sample Master List

Platform	Tasks
Facebook	• Check my bio statement to see if new information is needed. • Check new friend requests and accept as appropriate. • Update profile picture with headshot. • Check current group memberships and remove myself from groups that are no longer relevant. • Adjust my privacy settings.
LinkedIn	• Update my headshot. • Check current profile for accuracy and completeness and fill in any gaps from my current CV. • Add a section for my publications.
Instagram	• Update my headshot to one that shows my face more clearly. • Add new tagline I created to bio.
Twitter	• Update my headshot to one that shows my face more clearly. • Add new tagline I created to bio. • Update the people I follow to include professionals in my field/discipline.
Academia.edu	• Update my e-mail. • Cross-check the current list of citations with my CV to see if any are missing. • Update missing citations.
ResearchGate	• Update my e-mail. • Cross-check the current list of citations with my CV to see if any are missing. • Update missing citations.
Google Scholar	• Make sure my e-mail is up-to-date and verified. • Cross-check the current list of citations with my CV to see if any are missing. • Update missing citations.

want a complete set of items for each profile that you will be visiting. Use Table 5.2 to fill in your own task list or create your own table or spreadsheet for this purpose. If you visit the platform and realize that you forgot to include a task, just add it to your list.

Once you have your master list of tasks, you will have a better sense of what you need to compile to help complete the list. At minimum, you will probably need the following:

- A high-resolution headshot in multiple file sizes
- A current CV or résumé

TABLE 5.2
Master List Template

Platform	Tasks

- A tagline as discussed in chapter 4
- Bio statements of multiple lengths

Gather the materials you need in one digital space so that they are easy to refer to as you update your profiles and in case you need each of the items in the future (see Box 5.1 for an additional suggestion).

Before you get started with visiting your profiles, it may be necessary to update your CV or résumé. See the steps in chapter 6 if you have not already completed this task. Similarly, if you have not taken the time to craft your bio statements and tagline, refer to chapter 4 so that you have everything you need to get started.

Security

While you work your way through each profile, it is also a good idea to refresh your passwords on each platform. Best practice is to have a separate password for every profile; a password manager software product like 1Password (https://1password .com) or LastPass (www.lastpass.com) can help you keep all your passwords organized and easy to find. Typically, password manager software will have one master password that you use to get into the program where all your other usernames and passwords are housed, so you just need to remember one password to access everything else. Password manager systems will also allow you to generate random passwords that can help keep all your profiles more secure. In many password management applications, your passwords are securely stored in the cloud, so that when you update an

BOX 5.1.

Storing your information in the cloud.

To make sure the information you need for each platform is conveniently available to you, I recommend creating a series of folders (one labeled for each platform) in a cloud-based location such as Dropbox, Box, or Google Drive that can be accessed from anywhere that you have the Internet. If you ever decide to join a new platform and need a version of your headshot in a size that you used for a previous platform, it will be easy to locate. You can also store the most recent version of your CV or résumé as well as any other relevant documents so that they are handy and available if you need to post them in other online spaces.

account, that username and password can be updated on all your devices at the same time. Many password management software applications can connect with Internet browsers for easy password retrieval and also have apps that can be used on your smartphone or other mobile devices.

Accountability

One of the most effective ways to make sure you complete your full set of digital updates without flagging partway through is to set up an accountability system. The following sections explicate some potential options that might work for you.

Set a deadline.
Choose a date in the future when you want to have all your digital renovations completed and then work backward to schedule tasks from your master list. This method is most helpful if you have an event, such as going on the job market, promoting a book, or launching a new project that will necessitate going through and updating your online profiles.

Find a buddy.
Talk to your friends and colleagues to see if anyone else is considering updating their online profiles and wants an accountability buddy to get the work done. At the very least, you can reach out to me on social media and let me know that you are starting the process—I will be happy to check in and see how things are going! There is also a #AcDigID (for academic digital identity) group on Twitter that meets to hold regular "tweet chats" (see more about these in chapter 8) if you want to connect with a larger group that is interested in issues of digital identity for academics and higher education professionals.

Ask for help.
Involving someone else in your digital updating project is a great way to hold yourself accountable for getting things done. For example, if you need assistance with

launching your professional website, ask a tech-savvy friend or colleague to help you with the tasks outlined in chapter 7. Sometimes working with someone else on a project can just make it more fun.

Schedule regular sessions to do the work.
Choose a time of day (early morning, lunchtime, after work) when you can cross off some of the tasks on your master list. You can choose to tackle one profile per session or do smaller tasks that will add up over time. Making time on your calendar ensures that you will prioritize the process and make sure it gets completed.

Motivation

Getting started with your digital updates is only half the battle. You need to stay motivated so that you complete all your tasks and do not leave your profiles only partially updated. The following sections detail some potential motivations that might help you if your energy starts to lag.

Have a clear reason for the updates.
Similar to the deadline-setting strategy discussed previously, if you are planning to go on the job market, or if you have another important reason for tidying up your digital profiles, this can serve as your motivation to work through all the tasks on your master list.

Schedule a digital updates retreat.
When I first started to renovate my online profiles, I launched the process over a long July Fourth weekend. Having several days to devote to the project was a great motivation to get as much done as I could in the time that I had. I was also able to get into the mind-set of thinking about my personal brand and that allowed me to develop some consistency across multiple profiles. The good news is that you do not need a long weekend or vacation for a digital update retreat—in fact, a normal weekend or a couple hours here and there will do just fine. Just make sure that you have your master list and all your materials ready to go before you get started.

Do not do too much at once and burn out.
If you have a long master list of tasks in front of you, be careful not to take on too much and overwhelm yourself with the process of your digital update. Take each profile one step at a time and, eventually, everything will get done.

Work with existing profiles first.
Rather than add to your plate from the beginning, work on revising and updating the profiles where you already exist before you decide to join or add any new platforms to your online presence. This can also ensure that you will not do too much too fast and create an online presence that is too overwhelming and time-consuming for you to maintain.

Make it fun.

Although refreshing your digital profiles involves work, it can also be fun to create your spaces online, decide how you want to represent your work, and see all your accomplishments listed in one space. Put on some upbeat music, cook a fun snack, and settle in to have some fun as you work on this project.

Celebrate the completion of tasks.

As you complete the update for each of your profiles, celebrate! Depending on the state of your online presence, it may have taken you a lot of work to get to this point and that should be recognized and applauded. Although some digital update projects can be completed over a long weekend, others might take several months. Whichever is the case for you, do not forget to celebrate when the first stage of your update is done and all of your profiles are accurate, complete, and representative of you and your professional life and work.

Share your profiles when they are ready.

Once you have a completed profile, share it with friends or colleagues by posting about it on social media, adding it to the signature in your e-mails, or just talking about it at work. Many academics and higher education professionals are always looking for good examples of online presence and they will welcome your examples.

Managing and Maintaining Your Online Profiles

There are many reasons why your online profiles will require regular updates. You may change jobs, get a promotion, publish a new article or book, extend your network, create a new project, or have another professional event occur that makes it necessary to change your profiles. A good example is when I began to host podcasts. To help promote the shows, and to share about these new projects in my professional life, I updated all of my online profiles to include information about how to find out more about the shows and download episodes. I also updated my profiles when I formed an LLC, and whenever I publish something new or when I have a new headshot that I can share, that necessitates updates as well.

For some people, one of the most challenging components of building a robust online identity is managing and maintaining profiles so that none of them are inaccurate or appear deserted. Perhaps the most important thing that you can do is to get in the mind-set of remembering that your online profiles need updating when you have a major professional change, especially those profiles you are not visiting and engaging with on a regular basis.

Strategies for Profile Maintenance

The following sections offer some strategies to build your online profile maintenance into a regular, and manageable, schedule.

Keep a master list of your profiles.
The last thing you need to worry about is remembering all the places that you exist online, so as you create or update your profiles, add them to a bookmarked folder in your browser so that they are all listed in one place. Alternatively, you could create a Google Doc or Google Spreadsheet that stores the link to each platform and the date of the last time you refreshed your profile on that platform. The initial list that you already created for the activities in chapter 3 (see Table 3.1) is a great place to start.

Add new profiles one at a time.
If you decide to add any new platforms to your list of places that you exist online, add them one at a time and complete each new profile entirely before moving on to the next one. Then make sure to add any new profiles to the master list that you have created.

Schedule updates.
Decide how often you want to update your profiles and then schedule that update into your calendar. The frequency of your updating will depend on the amount of change taking place in your professional life. For example, if you are publishing new articles every few months, then at least some of your profiles will need to be updated on that schedule as well. If you have already created a schedule for updating your CV or résumé (I recommend, at minimum, checking these documents every six months or so, but even greater frequency is often advisable), then you can just add your digital updates to this schedule as well.

Automate updates where possible.
Some platforms will remind you about updates that need to occur. For example, Google Scholar will e-mail you when it finds a new citation that it thinks belongs on your profile. That automated e-mail also serves as a great reminder to add that new citation into your CV and onto the range of digital platforms where you share publications. Not all platforms offer automated updates, but keep an eye out for those that do and sign up when you have the chance. See Box 5.2 for an automation tool for the tech savvy.

BOX 5.2.
IFTTT.

IFTTT, or "if this, then that" (https://ifttt.com), is a free online tool that allows users to create "recipes" to automate services between a range of other online tools. The website has created a range of "applets" to get you started with doing things like keeping your Facebook and Twitter profile photos synced, saving and sharing your Instagram photos across other social media platforms, and tracking your daily Fitbit activity in a Google spreadsheet. The possibilities are endless!

Tips for Staying Informed About New Platforms and Features

Given the changing nature of online platforms, you will also want to make sure that you are staying up-to-date with the latest platform additions and feature updates. The following sections offer tips for staying informed.

Stick with your platforms of choice.
You do not need to worry about knowing everything about every platform. Choose the ones that you are most interested in learning about and participating in and then pay attention to changes that occur in those online spaces. Many of these changes will be obvious when they occur because the platform wants you to start integrating the changes into your engagement.

Follow your platforms' blogs.
Once you have your favorite platforms narrowed down, check each to see if it has a blog where it is posting updates on the platform and its features. If a platform is releasing a new feature, this is where you will see it announced first. (See Box 5.3 for a list of platforms that regularly post to a blog.)

Follow the blogs of social media scheduling tools.
Even if you do not use a social media scheduling tool like Buffer, Edgar, or Hootsuite (more on these tools in chapter 8), you might still want to follow their blogs for regular updates and advice on engaging with various social media platforms. (See Box 5.4 for a list of social media scheduling tools that regularly post to a blog.)

Talk with colleagues about your online presence.
I have learned about some of my favorite online platforms and tools from colleagues who have recommended them to me. When you talk about your online presence, you can learn about how others are representing themselves online and learn about new platforms, features, and strategies that might also work for you.

BOX 5.3.
Blogs for social media platforms.

Twitter: https://blog.twitter.com
Facebook: http://newsroom.fb.com
LinkedIn: https://blog.linkedin.com
Pinterest: https://blog.pinterest.com/en
Instagram: http://blog.instagram.com/
Academia.edu: https://medium.com/@academia
Google+: https://developers.googleblog.com

BOX 5.4.
Blogs for social media scheduling tools.

Buffer: https://blog.bufferapp.com
Edgar: http://blog.meetedgar.com
Hootsuite: https://blog.hootsuite.com
Friends+Me: http://blog.friendsplus.me
Tailwind: http://blog.tailwindapp.com

By using the strategies in this chapter, you should be able to keep your profiles updated, maintained, and accurate throughout your career to ensure that your online presence is consistent, professional, accurate, organized, of good quality, and representative of your many accomplishments. In the following chapter, you will learn some of the strategies for representing yourself online through one of the most important components of professional identity: your CV and résumé. (See Box 5.5 for an example of one higher education professional who is confidently sharing her story online as her career progresses.)

BOX 5.5.
A love for online engagement.

Dr. Monica F. Cox
Department Chair, Engineering
The Ohio State University

Find Monica online:
Professional website: www.preparedtobeapioneer.com/
Twitter: https://twitter.com/monicafcox
Instagram: www.instagram.com/monicafcox
Blog: www.preparedtobeapioneer.com/blog

Monica has always been a bit of an outlier in her professional career. As a woman of color in engineering who also holds a leadership position at her institution, she is used to code-switching to communicate with a range of stakeholder groups both within and outside of the academy.

One area where Monica has always felt more authentic and free to be herself is online. In her Twitter, Instagram, and Facebook communities, as well as through her blog, Monica has been able to share her experiences and what she wishes she had known about academia from the beginning. She views social media as a space to harness the power of story and feels an obligation to share what she has learned with people who may not have the same opportunities.

As a very social person, Monica loves the speed of connecting with people online. She also finds it easier to reach out to people online since she can more easily learn something about a person based on their digital identity and this helps her better connect with them.

Since earning tenure and becoming a department chair, Monica has gained more confidence about telling her own story in both face-to-face and online environments, but her love for online engagement continues.

6

DESIGNING AN EFFECTIVE
DIGITAL CV OR RÉSUMÉ

What's the Difference Between a CV and a Résumé?

Depending on your current professional role and your future aspirations, you may find yourself needing both a CV and a résumé at some point in your career. The simpler of the two is the résumé, which is a shorter record of your education and professional experience that can be limited to one page but can sometimes stretch to two pages. (It is rare to see a résumé of more than two pages, but sometimes a longer document is specifically requested.) A résumé should include information about your degrees and education, professional work experience (including institution names, title of position, and length of employment.) and your contact information. Often someone requesting a résumé assumes that you will offer an abbreviated record of your previous work and experience. Because they are short documents, it is assumed that your résumé will be tailored to the position for which you are applying, the grant application you are submitting, or whatever purpose caused you to create the document.

A CV, or curriculum vitae, is a longer document that includes details about your publications, professional presentations, grants received, honors, professional association memberships, and other information that offers a more detailed and holistic picture of your work experience. For experienced academics and higher education professionals, a CV can be an extensive document of 20 to 30 pages or more. CVs can be a bit more challenging to organize because of the volume of information included in the document. A CV should also be tailored to the audience who will be reading it and does not need to include an exhaustive list of every one of your professional accomplishments and experiences.

Creating CVs and Résumés

One of the most important credentials you can offer someone who is looking for you online is a recent version of your CV or résumé. Although some websites offer a version of this (e.g., LinkedIn), posting a PDF version of your CV or résumé where it can be easily found is also advisable. There are a range of reasons that people might be interested in reviewing your CV or résumé, including, but not limited to, the following:

- They read something you wrote and want to see what else you have published.
- They are looking for potential candidates to fill an opening they have (see Box 6.1 for an example of how one academic's online presence led to a job offer).
- They are exploring options for a keynote speaker and want to see your presentation experience.
- They are looking for a grant collaborator and want to see if you have the experience level they need.
- They see you as a peer and want to compare your work experience and output to their own.
- They are looking for a mentor with expertise in your field or discipline.

BOX 6.1.
Getting a job offer based on online presence.

Elizabeth (Liz) Covart
Historian and podcaster

Find Liz online:
Professional website: https://www.elizabethcovart.com
Podcast: www.benfranklinsworld.com
Twitter: https://twitter.com/lizcovart

After graduating with a PhD in history, Liz was not quite sure what she wanted to do. Knowing that she did not want a traditional academic job as a professor, she chose the route of an independent scholar and freelance writer. She also began to curate a Twitter feed, post on a blog, and build a professional website to share her CV.

When Liz came across the medium of podcasting, she fell in love. She liked being able to learn during otherwise unproductive times. However, when she went looking for a podcast on history she liked, she came up short. After 18 months of research and preparation, she decided to launch her own.

Liz now hosts a popular podcast called *Ben Franklin's World*, which receives over 160,000 downloads per month and continues to grow. She reaches thousands of people each week to share about topics she is passionate about. Without her online presence, which has been boosted by her podcasting, Liz is sure she would not be where she is today.

Most recently, her podcast led to a job offer to be a digital projects editor at the Omohundro Institute of Early American History and Culture, a research institute affiliated with the College of William & Mary.

When thinking about the audience for your CV or résumé, it is also important to note that these documents can be viewed differently across cultures. The American version of a résumé may not be perceived in the same light in European countries, for example (see Dunleavy, 2015b, for more on this).

Before you continue with the chapter, take a moment to list the top three ways that you plan to use your CV or résumé in the next year:

1. _____

2. _____

3. _____

Now, read the rest of the chapter with these goals in mind to create the best document(s) to help you meet those goals.

Common Components of Résumés

Shives and Sanders (2013) offer three formats for a résumé: chronological, skills-based or functional, or a combination of the two. For résumés that are chronologically organized, you will want to list your degrees and work experience in reverse chronological order. For résumés that are organized in a skills-based or functional format, you will choose areas of your expertise that are specifically related to the need for the résumé (whether a job application, a grant proposal, or another purpose) and focus specifically on the skills that the audience is asking that you demonstrate. A combination of the two formats can also be helpful if you do not have much formal work experience but have picked up a lot of skills throughout your graduate education or other life experiences. More detailed information about the typical content areas included in résumés is offered in the following sections.

Contact information.
This category should include your home address, your telephone number (cell phone number is fine), and a personal e-mail (make sure the address listed is appropriate for professional correspondence). Typically, contact information is listed at the top of the front page of the résumé and your name and a page number is listed in the header or footer of the following page, if applicable.

Education/degrees earned.
The first section of most résumés lists your education experience and your degrees. In this section, you will list, in reverse order, the degrees that you have earned. Some people also include certifications in this area, but given the brevity of a résumé, that information is better saved for a longer CV unless directly applicable to the audience for the résumé. If you have written a dissertation to earn your PhD, some people include the title of the dissertation in this area as well.

BOX 6.2.

Résumé example for multiple roles at the same institution.

Smithtown University—Smithtown, Iowa	
Director, Center for Theater Studies	January 2014–Present
Associate Director, Center for Theater Studies	July 2012–December 2013
Assistant Director, Center for Theater Studies	January 2011–June 2012

Work experience.

This section represents the main content of the résumé and will probably take up the most space. In this section, you will list all your professional experiences (i.e., the jobs that you have held). If you have worked in multiple roles at one institution, you will want to organize that information in such a way that those roles are clearly outlined (see Box 6.2 for an example of how to organize multiple roles from one institution).

Professional website address.

Given the lack of space available on a résumé, if you have a professional website, it is recommended that you include this information along with the rest of your contact information, so that the reader can look there for additional information about you if desired.

Because of their brevity, résumés are simple but powerful documents. They should be crafted with care and intentionality to ensure that you are offering the information that the audience of the document has requested.

Common Components of CVs

When it comes to designing your CV, there are a range of components that could potentially be included (see Box 6.3). Some of these components are useful to know regarding just about any position in higher education; these are the components that you will see included in most CVs that you will come across. Other components are those that might be useful but are more dependent on specific kinds of positions that one might hold. For example, a career administrator may not have teaching experience, grant funding, or conference presentations to include. On the other hand, she may have all those roles as part of her professional experience. This is why each CV is very personal and unique. In the following, I provide descriptions of each of the components (listed alphabetically) in more detail, but keep in mind that there may be other components that you will want to include that are more specific to you, your work experience, and your professional goals (a good example of this from my own CV are the sections I have added on the podcasts that I host and the webinars I facilitate).

BOX 6.3.
CV components (listed alphabetically).

Citizenship status	Professional affiliations
Conference and other presentations	Professional website address
Contact information	Publications
Continuing education	References
Education/degrees earned	Service work
Grants or funding received	Summary statement
Invited talks	Teaching experience
Languages spoken	Volunteer work
List of skills and/or competencies	Work experience

Citizenship status.
This component is often included at the end of a CV (and sometimes a résumé if space permits) and states whether you are a citizen of the country in which you are residing or whether your citizenship status is elsewhere.

Conference and other presentations.
In this section, you will want to include the various professional presentations that you have facilitated. Depending on your work, this section might include conference presentations, presentations for other institutions, workshops (internal or external to your institution), webinars or other online presentation mediums, and/or other presentation formats specific to your professional experience. If you have a large number of presentations, this section can be subdivided for ease of reading, or you can choose to label this section "Selected Presentations," which implies that you have more than you are listing and the ones you have included are those you consider to be the most pertinent.

Contact information.
Similar to a résumé, this category should include your home address, your telephone number (cell phone number is fine), and a personal e-mail (make sure the address listed is appropriate for professional correspondence). Typically, contact information is listed at the top of the front page of the CV and your name and a page number is listed in the header or footer of any following pages.

Continuing education.
If you have pursued education outside of your formal degrees, you can list those opportunities on your CV to help readers understand your range of experience and skill sets. This section might include individual courses you have taken (including massive open online courses, or MOOCs), certifications you have pursued through a professional organization or through your institution, institution-specific training

(e.g., leadership or management programs), or other ways in which you have pursued skills and knowledge outside of a formal degree program.

Education/degrees earned.
In this section, you list, in reverse order, the degrees that you have earned. Some people also include certifications in this area (although that might also belong in the continuing education section). If you have written a dissertation to earn your PhD, some people include the title of the dissertation in this area as well.

Grants or funding received.
If pursuing grants and external funding is part of your work experience, or if you have received institution-specific funding to support your research or other professional endeavors, those experiences can be listed on your CV in this section.

Invited talks.
Invited talks, such as keynotes, can be listed in a separate section from conference and other presentations, but this depends on the volume of items that you have in each category. In some cases, it might be easier to combine the sections and just note the appropriate presentation category with each item.

Languages spoken.
If you speak more than one language, you can include that information, as well as your proficiency level in speaking and reading that language, in this section.

List of skills and/or competencies.
Depending on the use of your CV, some people like to include a list of skills or competencies (e.g., software they are familiar with). This section is highly personalized and is usually included when responding to a job ad for a specific position that requires unique skill sets or competencies. When space permits, sometimes this section is also included on a résumé.

Professional affiliations.
If you are a member of professional organizations, you can list the organizations and length of affiliation in this section. If you hold an office within a professional organization, consider listing that information in your CV under the service work section (more on this in a moment).

Professional website address.
If you have a professional website, you can include this information in your CV along with the rest of your contact information. This information is typically included on the first page.

Publications.
If part of your professional experience includes writing and publication, you can include a list of these items in your CV. Depending on the number of items in

this list, this is another area where you may want to create subcategories for ease of reading. For example, my CV includes subcategories for books, edited collections, peer-reviewed articles, book chapters, and book reviews. There may be additional categories for your own writing.

References.

Some people choose to include references within their CVs. If you are posting the document online for all to see, I would recommend not including this information (and especially not including your references' contact information) without their consent. Many online job application sites now ask you to provide reference information separately, so it is becoming less common to include this information in your CV or résumé.

Service work.

Depending on your professional experience, you may have committee or task force involvement, advising, mentoring, or other roles to include in your CV. In this section, you will want to include a descriptive title for each opportunity as well as the length of time that you were involved.

Summary statement.

Some CVs include a summary statement at the beginning of the document that offers an overview of your professional experience and areas of expertise. This can also be included on a résumé if space permits. Although this can be a helpful addition to your CV or résumé, you will want to be careful that you do not include too much jargon or overgeneralizations that are often included in these kinds of statements, such as "team player" or "detail oriented." See Box 6.4 for an example of a summary statement I have used in my own CV (and that I have also included in my LinkedIn profile).

Teaching experience.

If teaching experience has been part of your work life, then this section can include the courses that you have taught, the institutions where you taught them, and the level (undergraduate or graduate) of students enrolled in the courses. Depending on the amount of teaching experience that you have, you may want to organize

BOX 6.4.
Example summary statement.

Nimble and creative higher education administrator with extensive experience in faculty development initiatives, course design and curriculum development, assessment, public speaking, and academic writing productivity and support. Known for developing strong collaborative partnerships within and across institutions to support faculty professional development initiatives and grant writing. Proven track record of relationship-building, innovation, and follow-through.

information in this section by institution, student level, or discipline. Remember that course numbers vary across institutions, so it is best to include the title of the course along with the course number. If you have experience teaching across modalities (online or hybrid/blended courses) that information can be noted along with each course as well.

Volunteer work.
If you are an active volunteer with any organizations outside of the service work that you perform as part of your professional role, this information can also be included on a CV. Keep in mind that some volunteer work, especially of a political or religious nature, can be interpreted in a range of ways, so consider how your volunteer work may be perceived by the different people who will be reading your CV.

Work experience.
In this section, you list all your professional experiences (i.e., the jobs that you have held). Because you have more space in your CV than in a résumé, if you have worked at a range of institutions, you may want to include a brief statement about each institution (including its enrollment size, geographic location, and any other information you believe is pertinent to the role you had there; see Box 6.5 for an example). As with a résumé, if you have worked in multiple roles at one institution, you will want to organize that information in such a way that those roles are clearly outlined. Some people also choose to include a bulleted list of accomplishments for each position that they have held; because of the additional details offered, this is something that would be more appropriate to a CV than to a résumé.

Organizing Your CV and Résumé

There are several right ways to organize your CV and résumé, so do not be concerned about doing it wrong. If you have a range of professional experiences, your organizational structure will depend on how you are using the CV and résumé. For example, in some cases, you will want to list your work experience in reverse chronological order,

---

BOX 6.5.
Example of brief statement describing institution of employment.

Smithtown University—Smithtown, Iowa

Smithtown University is a liberal arts institution that specializes in journalism and theater. As director of the Center for Theater Studies, I managed three staff members and a $200,000 budget and worked with faculty and administrators across the campus to provide opportunities for collaboration and professional growth for Smithtown's theater community. I also taught for Smithtown's world-renowned theater department.

with your most recent position listed first. In other cases, you may want to group like positions so that people can see where you had administrative roles with particular emphases on project management, collaboration, or strategic planning. As you organize your CV and résumé, there are some general best practices to keep in mind.

Plan to Create Multiple Versions

It can be helpful to have what you consider your "master" document with all of your experience, publications, presentations, and so on, so that you can pick and choose from the master when you are creating a more specific CV or résumé for a particular purpose. In the same way that you create a unique cover letter for all jobs that you apply for, you will also create a unique CV or résumé for different jobs, grant applications, and other professional opportunities that require a CV or résumé. In part, this is because different opportunities may have different length requirements for your CV or résumé (e.g., many grant "bio sketches" are limited to five pages), but unique documents will also be required because you probably have a wide range of experiences that are not all applicable for every circumstance.

Allow for White Space

One of the common challenges for CVs and résumés is to keep them visually easy to read. In some of the most disorganized CVs and résumés that I have seen, the author attempted to squeeze as much information as possible into the document without considering the reader's need to process the information being presented. By allowing the information on your CV or résumé to spread out, you create an easier reading experience for the person reviewing the document. This is also another argument for having a professional website (more on this in chapter 7), which allows you to offer additional information to the audience of your CV or résumé without including it in the document itself. (See Box 6.6 for an additional tip on CV and résumé spacing.)

Do Not Include Everything

For those with extensive professional experience, the word *selected* will become an important component in your CV or résumé. Rather than list every publication, presentation, and service obligation you have ever had, you can label each section as "Selected" to indicate that you are choosing only the most relevant information to

BOX 6.6.
CV and résumé spacing.

To ensure that the spacing on your CV or résumé is uniform, consider using the tables feature in Microsoft Word when building the document. You can enter information into the table and then remove the lines in between each cell so that the spacing is consistent but the table is not an obvious component of the document.

include there. Importantly, this practice should be applied with caution to your work experience, where not including everything could leave a gap that might raise questions for those who are interested in hiring you. Before you delete any of your work history, consider if it might be relevant to the reader or if it might raise questions by not being included. In the case of employment that you had while in graduate school, unless you have just graduated I recommend keeping only the information on your CV or résumé that is most pertinent to your current professional goals.

Do Not Use a Template

At one time, the Microsoft Word templates for organizing a CV or résumé were frequently recommended. Unfortunately, it is now quite obvious when you have built a CV or résumé from a template. Plus, using a template does not always allow for the flexibility to include all the elements that are related to your professional experience. Rather than use a template, applying the following guidance may help if you are starting from scratch:

- Place your name at the top of the first page of the document in a slightly larger font (it can be centered, flush left, or flush right).
- Place your contact information underneath your name.
- Use a consistent font throughout the document.
- Include page numbers and your name in the header or footer on all pages following the first page in case the document pages are somehow separated from one another.
- For your CV, organize the information in the document in the order that you think the reader will want to see it. This may mean that your educational experience is included at the end rather than the beginning or that you place your publications or teaching experience at the front of the document.
- Write the document so that it is easy to read; this will mean including white space throughout and not trying to place too much information on one page.

Posting Your CV and Résumé Online

When you are placing your CV or résumé online, there are also some things to consider regarding how a digital document can differ from a more traditional document. Creating your CV or résumé as a PDF is recommended because it can be read on multiple platforms and viewed more easily on mobile devices. Some other considerations are important to consider as well if you plan to transition your CV or résumé to a digital format.

Hyperlinks

On a paper document, links to websites, your e-mail address, or other online resources related to your professional experience will not mean much, but when posted online, hyperlinks in your CV or résumé can be incredibly useful. Be careful not to overdo it, but consider hyperlinking your e-mail address, professional website (if you have one), and your publications (if you include them). Hyperlinks also allow you to add some extra resources to your CV or résumé such as a link to a video of you presenting (if you have one to offer) or links to teaching artifacts such as syllabi or assignments (if you have them posted online). Dunleavy (2015a) also provides ideas of what to hyperlink in a digital CV or résumé and includes audio files as another option.

CV or Résumé as a Web Page

Although having a downloadable copy of your CV or résumé is recommended, you may also choose to create a page on your professional website that offers your CV or résumé as content on the page itself. This is recommended if you want the content of your CV or résumé to be searchable on the web so that people are drawn to your professional website when they search for one of your publications, presentations, or another component of your professional experience. (For more on professional websites, see chapter 7.)

Accessibility

Whenever you post a document online, especially in a professional capacity, you want to make sure that document is accessible for all readers or viewers. In the case of your CV or résumé, you will want to make sure the document, especially if it is a PDF, is screen readable for those who may have visual or other impairments that require an assistive technology device. Software platforms like Adobe often include helpful tools to ensure accessibility, but you will want to make sure that your document uses a header function (which allows for easier navigation of the document by a screen reader) and that the document can be read as text (rather than as an image, which can happen with some PDFs).

Keeping Your CV and Résumé Updated

If you decide to put your CV or résumé online, either as a PDF document or as a web page, it will be important to keep it updated. At the very least, you should mark the document or web page with the most recent date that your CV or résumé was updated, so that people can see how recent the document or information is that you are providing. How frequently you update your CV or résumé will depend entirely on your professional experiences. I recommend scheduling some time into your calendar monthly, just to make sure that you do not forget to add anything. Whether committee service, a conference presentation, a new publication, or a new course you are teaching, you do not want to lose track of something as time passes.

Using the general guidelines in this chapter will help you to set up a well-organized CV or résumé. Visit the book's companion website (www.mypiobook.com) for additional examples of a range of CE and résumé documents.

7

BUILDING A PROFESSIONAL WEBSITE

Do I Need a Professional Website?

There are many reasons why you might want to consider creating your own professional space online and, given the ease of securing a domain name and building a website (see Grandy, 2015), there are now fewer and fewer reasons *not* to have your own professional website. Corbyn (2010) found that many academics seeking websites are those newer in their fields "who see it as a way to enhance their job prospects." Moreover, when you create your own website, you do not have to worry about re-creating it if you decide to change jobs or move to another institution. Given the ease of creating a professional-looking online space to promote your work and projects, I think it is important that all academics and higher education professionals consider creating and curating their own website.

Common Reasons for Professional Websites

In this section, I elaborate on some of the more common reasons that academics and higher education professionals might choose to create a professional online space to showcase their work and experience.

You want a stable online space that you can control.
Even if you choose to create profiles on a range of social media platforms and other online spaces, you are not assured that those platforms will be around five years from now. By creating your own website, you can ensure that your domain name and online space is stable and long term.

You have services, products, or publications that you want to promote.
If you are a speaker, an author, a consultant, a coach, or have another professional identity where you are providing services or products for sale, having your own website creates a space for people to learn about you, communicate with you, and purchase your services or products. Social media platforms offer a space for promoting yourself and your services and products, but they do not act as a home base for you to describe the range of things that you might want to promote to your audience. A professional website can serve that purpose for you.

You want to create an online portfolio for when you go on the job market.
Being able to direct potential employers to a professional website where they can
learn more about your professional experience, publications, or teaching philosophy
can take some of the pressure off including these areas in your CV and cover letter
when applying for jobs. A professional website can also serve as a repository for artifacts of your professional life if you want to create a portfolio of past syllabi, assignment examples, writing samples, or other components that showcase your work as an
academic or higher education professional.

You would like to have more aesthetic control over how you are represented online.
Social media platforms and other online spaces may have some options for changing
colors, images, and themes, but a professional website that you design can be more
highly personalized to your tastes. There are a variety of free themes that you can
choose from to ensure that your professional website represents you from an aesthetic
perspective.

If any of the preceding reasons for creating your own professional website have con-
vinced you to take the leap, or if you currently have a professional website that needs
to be revised or updated, this chapter should help you to decide what to include on
your website and get you started with setting one up that meets your needs and goals.
(See Box 7.1 for one example of a higher education professional who created a professional website that augments other areas of his professional online presence.)

What Content Should I Include in My Professional Website?

Your professional website should be tailored to the audience that you hope to draw
and there are several different kinds of content that you might want to include.
J. Smith (2013) offers a range of possible items for websites being built by job seekers,
including contact information, a brief bio, your CV or résumé, a summary of your
professional objective(s), work samples, results of your work, links to professional
associations or press releases about your work, a blog, videos or other media, and testimonials. Corbyn (2010) also notes the inclusion of feeds from social media profiles
as a possibility. You will also want to include a headshot so that you are recognizable
when people are searching for you.

The following sections include additional suggestions for the kinds of content
that you might want to include for a range of purposes.

You Are on the Job Market

If you are trying to share information with potential employers, you will want to make
sure that the most recent version of your CV or résumé is front and center on your
website. You might also want to have pages that describe your teaching experience;
your publications; your administrative experience; and/or your teaching, research, or
leadership philosophies depending on the kind of job you are hoping to secure.

BOX 7.1.
Professional websites as conversation starters.

Thomas J. Tobin
Higher education consultant, author, and speaker

Find Tom online:
Professional website: http://thomasjtobin.com
Twitter: https://twitter.com/ThomasJTobin
Facebook: www.facebook.com/thomas.j.tobin
LinkedIn: www.linkedin.com/in/drtomtobin/

When Tom created his first professional website in the mid-1990s, it served as a way to introduce himself to the world of academia when he was still a graduate student. He hand-coded the site in HTML and created a database to share some of what he was learning in his PhD studies in English literature. When people started contacting him to learn more about his work, he knew he was onto something. Fast-forward more than 20 years and several career shifts later, and Tom is still using the web to connect with colleagues, build relationships, and grow his network.

Rather than collect followers, Tom is focused on using his online presence, primarily on Twitter and LinkedIn, to facilitate conversations, create professional collaborations, and share resources. He prefers not to retweet and repost much content, but rather to add value through his own lens by recommending others' work that he admires and through providing original content like his comic book on copyright. Tom uses online platforms to build quality in-person relationships that he nurtures when he connects with colleagues at conferences and visits campuses for speaking and consulting.

Tom employs social media in order to continue connections and interactions in his "real" life, so that his online presence is a true reflection of who he is as a person. That means that he works hard to nurture permeable borders between his personal and professional online spaces. He sees online tools as a way to create, join, and nurture conversations that can lead to deep and meaningful relationships with colleagues.

You Are Selling a Service

If you are creating a professional website to promote yourself as a speaker, consultant, or coach, or if you are providing some other kind of professional service, you will want to place information about that service, your rates, and a biographical statement in a prominent place. When selling a service, people need to know why they would hire you over someone else, so offering examples of your services and testimonials from past clients are both helpful elements to include on your website. If you are a speaker, including titles, descriptions, and time frames for your talks can help visitors to your site to know if you are a good fit for their event.

You Are Promoting Your Scholarship

If you create a professional website to share information about your articles, blog posts, or a recent book publication, making sure that people know where to find your scholarship is going to be a fundamental component of your site. If you can include downloadable copies of your work, that will be important to highlight. For an academic book, information about where to purchase the book, bonus materials, and highlights of the book's content might be the site's focus (see Box 7.2 for a best practice tip on creating a website specifically for book promotion purposes).

Best Practices for Professional Website Design

No matter the purpose of your professional website, there are some general best practices to keep in mind.

Make navigation simple.

As you build your professional website, you will want to make sure that it is easy to navigate and to find information. There is nothing more annoying than visiting a website for a specific purpose and then not being able to find what you are looking for. To ensure that your navigation is easy to follow, you will want to keep the structure of your website simple. As you design your website, think about what your visitors will consider the most important information about you and then place that information within one or two clicks from the main page of the website.

Use your name.

When people search for you online, the easiest way for them to find you is if you use your name on your professional website, and especially if it is part of your domain. If a dot com is not available for your name (someone might have already grabbed

BOX 7.2.
Promoting your book through a website.

Depending on the amount of information you plan to share about an academic book that you have published, you may want to consider creating a separate website just for the book rather than housing the book information on a professional website about you. To see an example of this, you can check out the website for my second book (www.bcdworkbook.com) or the website for this book (https://mypiobook.com). Both websites house bonus materials for each book that would not have fit on my professional website. (Additional book promotion website examples can also be found in the bonus resources on this book's website.)

it), find another appropriate domain where your name is available. For example, because dot com was not available with the name Katie Linder, I use the domain name katielinder.work for my professional website. This makes sure that I am easy to find and the domain name is also easy to remember. (See Box 7.3 for several more examples of professional websites where names are used for the web addresses.)

Be easy to contact.
One of the most off-putting components of a professional website is when you cannot easily find how to directly contact the person. Create a contact page or place your e-mail address prominently on each page so that visitors know how to communicate with you if they have questions for you or want to share information. Including other online profiles on your website, such as your Twitter handle or links to your Facebook or LinkedIn pages, is also a good way to connect with people, but a direct e-mail address is the most important (see Box 7.4 for a best practice tip on avoiding getting spammed).

Keep your website up-to-date.
As mentioned in chapter 1, a strong digital identity is one that is accurate and up-to-date. Whether you are using your professional website to promote your services,

BOX 7.3.
Examples of professional websites.

The following are some examples of academics and higher education professionals who have created their own websites.

- http://jwild.co.uk/home
- http://andymiah.net/#technology
- https://markcarrigan.net
- http://wendycadge.com
- http://travisgrandy.com
- http://nyashajunior.com

For easy links to these websites and to see more examples, take a look at the bonus materials on the book's companion website.

BOX 7.4.
Avoiding spam.

To ensure that you will not be targeted for spam by bots that may scrub websites just to find e-mail addresses for spamming purposes, when you place your e-mail on your website, you can use a structure like the following: name [at] domain [dot] com.

scholarship, or professional experience, the accuracy of what you place on the site is important to ensure that visitors find what they are looking for and are not presented with any information that is now out-of-date or incorrect. This means that you will need to regularly update and curate the information on your professional website (more on how to do this is included in chapter 5).

How Do I Set Up a Professional Website?

Before you get started building your professional website, there are several components of which you should be aware, especially if you have never had your own website in the past. One of the best things you can do is reach out to people you know who have their own websites to learn more about their setup and their recommendations for the service providers they use. However, you need to understand some basic components before moving forward with setting up your site.

Domain Name

The domain name of your website is the address that people will use to find the site. For example, Wikipedia.com is a domain name. Google.com is a domain name. Every website available on the Internet has a domain name. Typically, you will purchase a domain name for one to two years and pay a monthly or annual fee. Most domain names are under $15 per year (see Box 7.5 for information on free domain names). Traditional top-level domains such as .com, .net, and .org are usually relatively inexpensive, but they are not always available for the name that you might want to use. There are also other domains that can be more personalized, but these are often more expensive. A good example of this kind of domain name is the one I use for my own professional website: katielinder.work.

One question that many ask when choosing a domain for their professional website is whether they should use their own name for this purpose. This is an important question given that names may be modified due to marriage or other changes in family circumstances. However, when people search for you online, they will often

BOX 7.5.
Free domain names and websites.

If you do not want to pay an annual fee to purchase a domain name, you have the option of choosing a subdomain that is free of charge. Some websites having their own domain names will allow you to create a subdomain. However, it is important to note that these sites may have limited features and you will have less control over the administration of the site. For example, wordpress.com is a website where you could create a subdomain. The web address would be https://your-name.wordpress.com. Typically, subdomains also come with limited web space from the subdomain provider.

begin with your name. Having a website domain name that includes your name will make you more easily searchable and more easily found. If you decide not to use your own name, you will want to try to choose a domain that will remain evergreen. For example, you will not want to choose a name that includes your current position title or status (i.e., as a graduate student) or a name that is too trendy. As you explore different options, consider looking to other professional websites of colleagues in higher education to see the domain names they have chosen.

As you are beginning to think about your professional website, one of the most important components will be your domain name, so you will want to brainstorm some options and then check to see if they are available. Take a few minutes to brainstorm some options in the space provided:

_____   _____

_____   _____

_____   _____

_____   _____

_____   _____

Once you have some ideas in mind for your domain name, you will want to check to see if those names are available for rent. You can do this through something called a registrar; common examples are Namecheap, Bluehost, or HostGator. Start by going to the registrar's website, where they will have a search feature called "who is" for you to utilize. If the domain name that you want is already taken, the registrar will probably offer you a range of other options that include alternative personalized domains. Checking the availability of a domain name is always free. After you have chosen a domain name and found it to be available, you can purchase the domain name through the registrar. After this purchase, they will send you a confirmation e-mail with additional information about your domain name. You will also receive annual reminders from the registrar to make sure your information related to the site is up-to-date, including your e-mail, physical address, and phone number (see Box 7.6 for privacy considerations when choosing a registrar).

Hosting Provider

Once you have a domain name, you will need to also rent web space. Sometimes, the registrar through which you purchase your domain name will also provide web space options for an additional fee. Some examples of registrars that offer both domain name and web space purchasing are GoDaddy, DreamHost, Squarespace, and Network Solutions, but there are many others. Reclaim Hosting (https://reclaimhosting.com) is another example of a hosting service specifically for students, faculty, and higher education institutions. You can also purchase a domain name and web space separately. Without web space, your domain name will be useful only as a redirect to another website with web space (see Box 7.7 for more information on redirects), so if you plan to tie content to the domain name you have purchased, you will need a hosting provider.

When purchasing web space, you will need to make choices regarding disk space (i.e., how much space you have for storing data), bandwidth (i.e., upload and download quotas for accessing that data), and the level of support you want to receive for your website (including uptime guarantees). At minimum, your professional website will need 20 megabytes (MBs) of space to exist, but many providers will offer you gigabytes (GBs) of space given that digital storage is now so inexpensive. Some hosting providers also offer e-mail addresses that are tied to your domain name, but this is not always a feature. Web hosting services are usually purchased on monthly or yearly plans; for a monthly plan, most hosting will not cost more than $20. You may also get a discount when paying on an annual basis. Your professional website should not

BOX 7.6.
Privacy considerations for choosing a registrar.

When choosing a registrar to purchase your domain name, you will want to consider the security features offered by the registrar. For example, some registrars offer a privacy option for your personal information where they replace your contact details with those of the registrar in regard to information such as e-mail, physical address, and phone number. This is a service that should be provided free of charge and will be clearly stated as part of the benefits of that particular registrar. If this service is not offered by your registrar, the personal contact information you provide in relation to the domain name will be publicly searchable.

BOX 7.7.
Redirecting domain names.

In some cases, you may want to purchase a domain name, or you may already own one, that will be used only for the purpose of redirecting. For example, my old professional website was kathrynlinder.com. When I rebranded my online presence to using my more informal name of Katie Linder, I needed a different domain name to reflect that. However, I had already circulated my older professional website address for several years. Once I purchased katielinder.work and transitioned my information to that site, I redirected kathrynlinder.com so that when people visited that domain name, they were sent to the new site. In this situation, kathrynlinder.com is not tied to any web space but is being used only as a redirect. Any domain name you are using as a redirect will still need to be purchased. A best practice with redirects is to use them only between websites that you own or to point visitors to your web profile on a site like Academia.edu or ResearchGate. It is important to note, however, that unless a website offers permission, web etiquette suggests that you should only redirect to another site that you own.

cost more than approximately $130 to $150 per year, which includes the cost of both your domain registration and web hosting.

Content Management System

Once you have your domain name and your web space, you will need a way to add information to your site. A common way to do this is through a content management system (CMS). A CMS works in a similar way to a learning management system, which you may be more familiar with. Most CMSs allow users to easily manipulate data (e.g., text, images, and other content) to build websites and web pages. Popular examples include WordPress and Drupal. To use a CMS, you need to install it on your web space. As this is a typical task for setting up a website, hosting providers will frequently offer additional information and support for how to do this. One feature that you can look for when choosing a hosting provider is whether they have created automated installation tools for CMSs.

Website Extras and Bonus Components

Once you have your professional website designed, there are a few other components of which you need to be aware.

Themes

CMSs like WordPress and Drupal also have "themes" that you can download and install into your website to give the site a particular look or feel. Although your site will most likely come with a theme, it is common to customize this feature of your website. Many themes are free for a basic package, but fee based for more advanced settings. The cost of advanced theme packages ranges from tens to hundreds of dollars depending on the features included. Sometimes this fee is assessed annually, depending on the support offered by the vendor. For most people setting up a professional website, the basic package will be fine, but if you want more control over the aesthetics or functionality of your site, you may want to consider purchasing a more advanced option (see Box 7.8 for more information on website design help).

Front-End Extensions

Sometimes called *widgets* or *add-ons*, front-end extensions are components that you can add to your site that will be seen by people who visit. These can include features like a counter of site visitors, a feed to your most recent social media posts, or a dynamic word cloud of all tags used in your blog posts. For front-end extensions, the list is almost endless. One of the best ways to decide what front-end extensions you want to include on your website is to visit other sites that you like and see what they have. Most front-end extensions are clearly labeled with a name or designer so that you can search for the extension and add it to your own site. Sometimes front-end extensions are tied to a specific CMS theme.

BOX 7.8.

Need website design help?

For people who are brand new to website design, some hosting providers offer helpful tools. For example, websites like Squarespace.com and Wix.com not only allow you to purchase a domain name and web space but also have tools to create web pages based on templates where users can easily add in content. If you are overwhelmed by the process of creating your own professional website, these resources may be a good place to start.

Alternatively, you can also hire someone to design and maintain your professional website. If you are looking to outsource this work, ask around to see if your colleagues have suggestions, or check the footers on the websites of academics or other professionals whom you admire. Web designers often link to their services in the footers of websites they have created.

If you decide to hire a website designer, a good practice is to ask to see samples of current websites that they have helped to build so you can review a portfolio of their work before hiring them. Most website designers will also provide you with a contract to document the work that is to be performed and the payment structure.

Back-End Extensions

Also called *plug-ins*, back-end extensions include components like back-up systems for your website's content and database; spam filters for comment systems; metrics for who has visited your site, clicked-on links, and where those visitors were referred from; and other administrative tools that can help your site function well. Back-end extensions are CMS specific and are frequently promoted inside the CMS on your website's design dashboard. You can also visit a CMS's main website to learn more about all of the different extensions that have been designed for that CMS.

Checking Your Website for Quality

There are a range of quality indicators that you can use to assess your professional website and ensure that it is meeting your needs and the needs of your audience. There are some website "graders" available by searching on the web, including a simple one from HubSpot (https://website.grader.com) that can be used to assess your website's overall quality. If you prefer to do this assessment yourself, there are some basic indicators of website quality.

User Experience

An effortless user experience is the foundation of a good website. This means that visitors can navigate your website to find what they are looking for, that they do not encounter problems like broken links, and that they are able to understand the basic functions of your website. You want to make sure that visitors to your website have the best experience possible and that they can find what they are looking for simply and easily. This can be more difficult than it seems, especially if your website includes a lot of content. Mapping your website content to choose the menu structure that will best meet your goals and the needs of your visitors is a good place to start to ensure a good user experience.

Accessibility

One component of user experience that I want to highlight is accessibility. You will want to be sure that your website is accessible to all audiences, including those with sensory disabilities. Many of the themes available within CMSs have accessibility already built in, but not all themes do. In WordPress, you can search for themes using this criterion, so that is a good place to start. Accessible websites are more easily read by screen readers and will also include things like alt-tags for photos and other visuals for visitors who have difficulty with vision. Accessible websites also include transcripts or closed captions on all audio and video content for visitors who have difficulty with hearing, so this is something you should consider when posting multimedia content. Building in accessibility to your website from the very beginning is the best way to ensure that this quality indicator is met.

Speed

When visitors come to your website, the last thing they want to do is wait for the pages on your website to load. The speed of your website is determined by a range of factors, including the CMS, the plug-ins you add to your website, and the theme that you choose. The content of your site can also be a factor. For example, if you have large page sizes and high-resolution images, that can influence the load time of your website. The speed can also be affected by the Internet speed of the person visiting your website, but that factor is out of your control. The speed of your site is also determined by the server where your website is hosted, so if speed is important to you, a dedicated server might be a good option to consider. For most people, shared hosting is perfectly fine for the typical professional website to give you the speed that will load your pages without noticeable delays. If you notice that your website is slow to load, common culprits can be your CMS theme or plug-ins, so start there with your troubleshooting.

Search Engine Optimization

Search engine optimization (SEO) is the level at which your site content is generally searchable by certain words and terms. For example, when I Google my own name, my professional website is the first result that is returned. This means that my SEO for that website in connection to my name is strong. In part, this is because I also have several other websites (for books, podcasts, and other projects) and social media profiles that link back to that site and that are also using my full name. One of the most important things to do on your website to increase your SEO in relationship to your own name is, perhaps not surprisingly, to use your own name on your website. For example, this might include choosing the name that people will use most frequently to search for you as your website's title (this is different from your website's domain name, which can also influence SEO), referring to yourself in the third person on your website's about page, and using your full name as your CMS username (rather than a generic "administrator") so that your full name shows up each time you post on your site's blog.

SEO is a complicated algorithm that takes into account the language used on your website, how many other websites link to yours around a particular topic, and how the coding on your website is optimized to connect to certain keywords or phrases. Although there are some existing tools, such as BrandYourself (https://brandyourself .com), that are meant to help improve your search results, it is important to know that each search engine calculates SEO differently, so it can be a bit of a black box in terms of trying to "game" the system to increase SEO to your website.

Mobile-Friendliness

Browsing websites on mobile devices such as smartphones and tablets has become increasingly common. However, not all websites are created so that they dynamically adjust to the different sizing requirements of these screens. If you have ever visited a website using a mobile device and found it to be almost unreadable because of how the text displays on top of images or other text, that is a good example of a site that is not mobile-friendly. Like the accessibility quality indicator discussed previously, many CMS themes are now building in mobile-friendliness to the foundation of their coding. This is a searchable criterion that you can use when choosing a theme, so that you do not have to worry about this quality indicator and can just focus on the content of your site.

Content

The final quality indicator that you should be considering for your professional website is related to the content of your site. You will want to ensure that there are no typos, broken links, low-quality images, or other distractions within your content that create a poor experience for your website visitors. The content quality of your site is closely tied to the need for an effortless user experience as previously discussed. Because poor-quality content will distract a visitor, these two quality indicators often go hand in hand and should be considered together.

Keeping Your Website Updated

Similar to other areas of your online identity, a professional website will need regular maintenance to ensure that all is performing as it should be. In particular, you may need to download updates to your CMS, themes, plug-ins, and more. Some of these updates will happen automatically depending on your CMS and the settings that you choose, but other updates will need to occur manually. You will also need to make sure that you continue to pay for your domain name and web space so that you do not lose either one. Your registrar will also contact you annually to update your registration contact information, including any changes to your physical address. Lastly, you might want to consider backing up the information on your professional website on a regular basis. This backup can be useful if your website is compromised with a virus or if somehow everything on your site is accidently deleted (it is easier than you think).

Like your digital CV or résumé, you will want to make sure that your professional website is always up-to-date. Consider scheduling updates once per month when you check your CV or résumé for updates so that you can make changes across all your digitally published content at the same time. About every six months or so, review the overall look and organization of your professional website to assess whether it is still meeting your needs and goals. If your goals have changed due to transitioning to a new position, the publication of a new book, or some other professional accomplishment, it is possible that your site may need a new theme with different functionality, a new organization for your menu structure, or some new pages with additional content.

The components of this chapter cover the basics of what you need to create your own professional website, but there are many other resources available to guide you. Visit this book's companion website (www.mypiobook.com) to find these resources and additional examples.

TWEETS, UPDATES, AND OTHER FORMS OF POSTING ONLINE

What You Need to Know About Posting Online

When you first start posting online, or when you decide to begin posting online in a more intentional way, it can be difficult to know where to start. To some degree, you learn about what works best for posting online to your specific audiences through trial and error. That said, there are some basic best practices that can help you decide the kinds of information that you want to post, how to post that information effectively, how to encourage engagement and response from your audience, and the frequency with which you should be posting. In the first part of this chapter, I provide answers to some general questions about sharing information that can be applied, for the most part, across a range of different platforms.

What Kind of Information Should I Post?

The kind of information that you choose to post online depends a lot on what you decide about where and how you want to be online (see chapters 2 and 4). In particular, you need to decide the ratio of content that you will want to post (see Table 8.1 for one spectrum of the kinds of content you can post online). Some people prefer to keep their posts online purely professional and will post only links, images, and information related to their own or others' work in their field. Most people post a mix of personal and professional, sharing about their meals out, things that inspire them, and accomplishments of their children. There are also some people who post online only about the personal and prefer not to take the risk of posting about anything related to their professional lives in case what they post is somehow misinterpreted.

There are several different kinds of updates that you can try.

Behind-the-scenes peeks.

If you are in the middle of a project, take a moment to post an update about what you are working on with a picture of your work space. These kinds of behind-the-scenes posts help people to get to know your work style and inform followers about your current projects.

TABLE 8.1
Spectrum for Personal and Professional Promotion of Online Content

	Self-promoting	*Other-promoting*
Personal	Sharing information about your personal accomplishments, such as completed workouts or day-to-day personal activities	Sharing information about your children's milestones, a friend's new business venture, or a link to a personally inspirational resource
Professional	Sharing information about your recent publications, professional accomplishments, or day-to-day professional activities	Sharing information about your colleagues' work, resources for your field, or links to interesting professional news and insights

Current status.
This is one of the more common kinds of updates and just lets your followers know what you are currently up to. Maybe you are making your way through a to-read pile, waiting to hop on a plane to attend a conference, or feeling excited about a great meeting with a colleague. All are fodder for current status updates.

Review of a product or service.
If you have recently had a good experience with a product or service related to your work, you can share about that with your followers. Make sure to include the handle for the company you are talking about, especially if it is your own institution that you are praising.

Accomplishments.
Sharing about your triumphs is a great way to allow your followers to celebrate alongside you, but be wary of the "humble brag"—if you have something you are proud of, you can openly say so. Common announcements in the academic community are successful thesis and dissertation defenses, the acceptance of an article for publication, a good teaching day, and other exciting professional news items.

Entertainment.
Some updates are meant purely for entertainment. You might post a funny story, a humorous GIF, or share something entertaining that someone else posted and that you thought others would also enjoy. There are several humor-based academic memes floating around and these are frequently shared across social media channels.

Asking for help or information.
If you are stuck on a problem, looking for a resource, or just have a general question, you can post an update that asks for help or information from your followers. This kind of crowdsourcing is becoming more common (for a range of examples, see Zoref, 2015).

BOX 8.1.

News aggregation websites.

- AllTop: http://alltop.com
- Futurity: http://futurity.org
- Holy Kaw: http://holykaw.alltop.com
- Reddit: https://reddit.com
- SmartBrief: http://smartbrief.com
- StumbleUpon: http://stumbleupon.com
- TED: https://ted.com

Sharing news or information.

Sharing links to news items or other information is a common update theme across social media sites. If you want to share content through social media but you are not sure where to find things that might be interesting and useful to your audience, there are several news aggregation sites online where you can find content to share (see Box 8.1 for a list of ideas).

Providing inspiration.

On most social media platforms, you will see quotations and other social media images that are meant to provide inspiration. There are even tools like Wikiquote and Wordswag to help create these kinds of images. See chapter 11 for more information on how to create social media images and the platforms and tools that are available to help you.

Deciding What Is Appropriate Information to Post Online

When thinking about the kinds of information that you choose to post online, the following guiding questions can help you decide what is appropriate for you:

- Would it be all right for my boss or coworkers to see this post?
- Would it be all right for my immediate family members to see this post?
- Would it be all right for my extended family members to see this post?
- Do I mention anyone specifically in the post? If so, would it be alright if he or she were to see the content of the post?

As you can see, most of these questions are related to how you think the content that you will be posting will be perceived by others. Although you cannot control how everything you post will be perceived, it is helpful to consider whether you would say to people face-to-face what you are posting in other settings. The Internet is a tempting place for rants because it feels more anonymous, so it is important to consider that almost nothing is anonymous online.

If you spend any amount of time on social media, you will also see your share of snarky, sarcastic, and downright negative posts about a range of topic areas (and people). In my opinion, those kinds of comments serve to bring everyone down and do not help in building a positive reputation for you either personally or professionally. Although I am not arguing for a squeaky-clean Internet space, I always recommend thinking about whether what you post will be helpful, entertaining, or useful in some way to your audience. If the goal of your post is merely for you to let off steam about a topic or issue that you are upset about, think twice before posting it.

Take a moment to consider the kinds of things that you are most interested in, and write down some ideas for content that you could share on the platforms where you have profiles:

_____

_____

_____

_____

_____

_____

_____

_____

What Makes an Effective Post?

The effectiveness of your post depends on the requirements of the platform on which you are posting, but some general features are almost always appreciated:

Cite your sources.
If you are posting a link or information about someone else's ideas or content, it is always appreciated when you cite the original source. This not only is respectful to the author of the content but also makes it easier to find the resource if your post is shared, retweeted, or otherwise passed on to others who might not know you.

Use the right hashtag.
If you are posting information that is helpful or of interest to a specific community, see if that community has a hashtag so they can more easily find the information you are posting (more on hashtags later in this chapter).

Include a short link.
Long, unwieldy links are not aesthetically pleasing, so if you are including links in your posts, shorten them so they are not a distraction for the reader (more on short links later in this chapter).

When appropriate, include an image.
To help make your post stand out, it is now becoming necessary that you include an image. Many platforms display posts on a scrolling screen, so if you have an image with your post, it is more likely to be noticed by someone and not passed by.

How Can I Get More Followers?

Generating followers on social media platforms requires a long-game approach. Sometimes people will need to see several posts from you that interest them before they decide to follow you. Other times, people will follow you because they are introduced to you by someone else on the platform. The more you engage with online platforms, the more opportunities people have to find you, interact with you, and decide that they like the content you are producing and sharing. Think about the reasons you follow the people that you do. Most of the time, you are related to them, you know them in real life (IRL), or they produce something that you find entertaining, helpful, or useful. If you are producing regular, quality content online and intentionally and genuinely engaging in communities that are of interest to you (and using their hashtags) then you will increase your followers over time. You may also see boosts in your followers after specific events, like professional conferences where you might be more likely to be posting more frequently (see chapter 9 for more about engaging in communities online).

Should I Engage With My Students Online?

As technologies are becoming more embedded into our pedagogical practices, the question has shifted from *whether* to engage with your students online to *how* you should engage with your students on online platforms. If you are on any form of social media, your students will find you and attempt to interact with you in those online spaces. Choosing how to engage with your students online may be impacted by institution- or department-specific policies where you work, so check for those first. If no policies exist, you will need to decide in what capacity you want to engage with your students online. If you want to keep things professional, consider connecting only with students on platforms such as LinkedIn, Academia.edu, or ResearchGate, where most communications are of a professional nature.

If you do want to connect with students through online platforms for pedagogical purposes (Twitter and Facebook are both examples of platforms frequently used in classrooms), consider placing guidelines for your engagement on that platform in your course syllabus so that students will know what to expect. There are a couple of important things to keep in mind when you are engaging with students online (also see Box 8.2 for one academic's choices regarding engaging with students online).

Not all students are on social media.
Some students prefer not to engage on social media, so if you are making online engagement a classroom requirement, consider an alternative assignment for students who do not want to create online accounts on those platforms.

You set the boundaries.

As the person in power and the authority figure for your students, you get to set the boundaries of where and how you want to engage with your students online. Remember that you can always decline an invitation from a student on a platform where you do not want to connect. For more on engaging with students via social media for pedagogical purposes, see Joosten (2012).

How Can I Get User Interaction With My Posts?

A lot of posts on the Internet can feel like they are going into a black hole, especially if no one comments on them, retweets or likes them, or otherwise acknowledges their existence. The following general ideas can help encourage more active engagements with your posts.

BOX 8.2.

Modeling professional online engagement for students.

Jeff Jackson
Director of curriculum evaluation
Long School of Medicine at UT Health San Antonio

Find Jeff online:
Twitter: https://twitter.com/jeffjackson
LinkedIn: www.linkedin.com/in/txjackson

Early in his career, Jeff was pretty open online, often connecting with current and former students to help model how to be a digitally engaged academic. Once his son was born, however, Jeff became more private online and now regularly audits his connections and privacy settings to make sure that what he is sharing online is being seen by the people he intends.

Over time, modeling professional online engagement has become more formalized as Jeff now trains students, often at new-student orientations, about how to engage online in a professional way. Since he works at a medical school, Jeff emphasizes that mistakes about what you put online can be career ending.

He always advises students that images posted online often do not include the context, and they can inadvertently be damaging and impact one's educational and career success. Cameras in mobile devices, as well as the ability to take screenshots of online postings, have created an environment where all actions, no matter how brief, can be shared with university administrators via e-mail or otherwise.

Jeff has no illusions about online privacy and wants to make sure the students he works with also have a realistic understanding about what it means to share their personal and professional lives in online spaces.

Ask questions.
By asking a question, you are inviting people to respond to something specific and they are more likely to engage with you.

Include hashtags.
Posting something to a specific community can encourage more engagement with your post because it is directed to a particular audience.

Ask people to comment.
Directly requesting interaction from people to one of your posts increases the likelihood that people will take the time to say something.

Include contact information.
If you truly want people to engage with you, tell them how by including an e-mail address, your Twitter handle, or information about how to connect with you on other social media platforms.

Share your passions.
Sharing your passions means that other people with that same passion will find you and will want to interact with what you have to say.

Be honest and genuine.
If you choose to be open, honest, and genuine about your life, people will most likely respond because they will be able to relate to your experiences.

How Do I Respond to Negative Interactions With My Posts?

Inevitably, no matter how hard you try, someone will not like something that you post online and they will tell you. Sometimes this feedback can be helpful. Maybe you have posted something that is incorrect or partially inaccurate and the person is offering a correction. In this case, expressing gratitude and updating your post is the best response. Other times, the person may have misperceived what you had intended to say and a clarification response can be helpful. In a small number of cases, someone may interact with you just for the purpose of being mean. These people are termed *trolls* and intentionally try to provoke fights and arguments in online environments. Because of the complexity of the topic of online conflict, I have devoted an entire chapter to responding to negative interactions happening to you or others (see chapter 10 for more information).

How Frequently Should I Post?

Although each platform has its own posting frequency etiquette, a general rule is to not post more than four to five times per day per platform (keeping in mind that you may post the same content across multiple social media sites). Many social media platforms now employ algorithms that show only a certain number of your posts to followers. How frequently you post will also depend on the amount of information that you have to share and if, for example, you have prescheduled evergreen content on any of the platforms where you post regularly. (Evergreen content is not time specific and will not expire; this means it can be posted numerous times on the same platform over a period of weeks, months, or years.) Because I post a lot of evergreen content across multiple social media platforms each day using a social media scheduling tool called Edgar (more on this later in the chapter), I feel less pressure to be posting real-life updates. That said, people choose to follow you on social media platforms because they want to hear from you and get updates on what you are up to. To keep from constantly checking in on social media, some people choose to engage with social media at certain times of the day like early morning, the lunch hour, or after work so that they can post an update, reply to other people's comments on earlier updates and posts, and comment or "like" the posts from people they follow.

One best practice is to choose a ratio of the kinds of posts you plan to make and then stick to it so that your followers have a sense of regularity. For example, you might choose to make personal posts about half the time and professional posts the other half. Or you might decide you want to post 60% evergreen content and 40% real-time updates. Of course, these ratios are general estimates, but they can help you decide on a day-to-day or weekly basis if you have been posting what you feel is appropriate on the platforms you have chosen. If you have lots of content to share, especially if that content is of your own creation, consider being more strategic about when you post certain items to your various platforms so that it does not seem like you are just on social media to promote your own work. You will also want to make sure that you are sharing other people's content and the resources that you have found helpful as much, if not more, than you share your own content and resources (if you are interested in the topic of building a brand for self-promotion, see the information included in chapter 11).

Helpful Tools for Posting Online

Whatever you choose to post online is contributing to the story you are telling about your life and work. Indeed, in *Storybranding*, Signorelli (2012) argues,

> Technology is providing us with a great number of high-touch storytelling channels. Social networks like YouTube, Facebook, and Twitter are, in effect, storytelling portals. Questions such as "What's on your mind?" or "What's happening?" provide open invitations for users to tell stories about their lives. (p. 25)

Moreover, there are many online tools that allow you to tell a continued story over time, or to tell your stories more easily.

BOX 8.3.
Academic and higher education hashtags.

Raul Pacheco-Vega (www.raulpacheco.org) has curated a list of some of the more popular social media hashtags for academics and higher education professionals (Pacheco-Vega, 2013). Here are a few of my favorites:

- #PhDChat—a hashtag to discuss issues and topics related to getting a PhD
- #ScholarSunday—a hashtag to share favorite scholars whom you follow each week
- #ECRchat—a hashtag to connect early career researchers
- #AcWri—a hashtag to discuss topics and issues related to academic writing

For example, hashtags (always used with a # symbol followed by a word or phrase) can be used to "tag" posts on almost any platform so that anything that uses that hashtag is grouped together (see Box 8.3 for hashtags that have been created for specific academic and higher education communities). Indeed, when I was working on this book, I created a hashtag for my 10-day writing retreat called #10dayswriting that I used to tag posts on Twitter, Instagram, Facebook, and videos that I posted to YouTube. Similarly, many academic conferences will create a hashtag for their event and encourage "live-tweeting" or use of that hashtag to post regular social media updates on Twitter and other social media platforms (see Box 8.4 to learn about one higher education professional who is a prolific live-tweeter). This use of the hashtag encourages online community-building for the people attending the event and draws in an audience of people online who may not have been able to attend the conference or event face-to-face. Unless someone else starts using the hashtag that you create (which is a good argument for creating something unique and checking on various platforms to see if it is already in use), your record of posts connected to that hashtag will always exist on those platforms. It has also been found that on certain platforms, such as Instagram and Twitter, posts with at least one hashtag have more engagement on average (Parker, 2016). If Instagram is your platform of choice, services like Instatag and TagsForLikes can tell you the most popular hashtags on that specific platform.

TweetDeck is another tool that can help you lead or paticipate in "tweet chats" or live conversations that occur on Twitter through the use of a hashtag. In tweet chats, people come together on Twitter at a predetermined date and time, have a conversation about a topic or issue, and label all their tweets with the same hashtag so that people can follow along. This conversation is usually led by someone who is posting questions (labeled "Q1," "Q2," etc.) that are answered by conversation attendees (labeled "A1," "A2," etc.). This conversation can then be archived as a blog post and shared more widely with others who could not attend in real time. (Other tools, like TChat and Twubs, are also helpful when leading or participating in a tweet chat.)

Another set of helpful online tools for posting to a range of platforms are social media schedulers. These tools allow you to precreate content, schedule when you

BOX 8.4.
Live-tweeting conferences and events.

John Robertson
Digital education librarian
Seattle Pacific University

Find John online:
Professional website: www.kavubob.com
Twitter: https://twitter.com/kavubob
LinkedIn: www.linkedin.com/in/rjohnrobertson

For John, academic engagement at conferences is all about sharing, and one of the ways he does this is through Twitter. John is one of the best live-tweeters I know. This may be in part because of his commitment to open educational resources, which are created for the explicit purpose of sharing.

When John attends a live event, he listens for sharable content, summarizing main points from speakers, sharing out resources, and retweeting and sharing others' comments and ideas. He enjoys making connections between his own experience and a wider audience through the conference back-channel.

Over time, John has honed his live-tweeting strategies. John views his attendance at conferences as a privilege and tries to create an inclusive online back-channel where others can virtually experience the live events. He retweets with the explicit purpose of raising other people's voices.

Twitter is one platform where John contributes to a larger ongoing conversation in his field and where he can make personal connections to people he meets at face-to-face conferences, whether they are there in person or connecting with him virtually.

would like for it to post, and then choose the platform where you would like it to be released. Some common examples are Hootsuite, Buffer, Friends+Me, Tailwind, Post Planner, Sprout Social, and Edgar. These tools also allow the possibility to "batch" the creation of your social media content, which is especially helpful if you do not have time to regularly post throughout the day but would still like to be sharing links, resources, and information online on a consistent basis.

There continues to be some controversy surrounding social media scheduling, although this may be waning as more people automate their posts. A main concern is that social media scheduling is a less genuine way to post online and that you are carefully curating your posts, it is easier to post something that is an artificial representation of your life. Although I see this point, I can also appreciate the ease of prescheduling posts about things like favorite podcasts I want to share, an article link that I found helpful, or a link to a previous podcast episode or blog post that I created and want to make sure that people are reminded of. This kind of content is evergreen and it does not really matter when you post it. It will not become less genuine over time. More real-time content, such as updates on a sports event or tweets related to a conference or other live event, are obviously better when they are posted in the moment.

Social media scheduling tools can certainly help you to save time and make your social media posting more efficient. For example, I use Edgar to create posts for Twitter, Facebook, and LinkedIn that post to six different Twitter accounts, four Facebook pages and one Facebook profile, and one LinkedIn profile (Instagram does not allow prescheduled posting that is automated—if it did, I would do that too!). Altogether, I am managing the content for 12 different social media accounts. If I tried to create real-time posts for all of these accounts, I would spend my entire day generating and managing posts on these social media platforms. Through social media scheduling, I am able to post automated content multiple times a day and then add in a couple posts here and there on my platforms of choice (mostly Twitter, Facebook, and Instagram) that are real-time updates.

A final helpful tool to be aware of if you plan to post a lot on various social media sites is the URL shortener. Tools at bit.ly, Buffer, goo.gl, tinyurl.com, and Hootsuite allow you to take longer links and shorten them while still maintaining the direct connection to that link's content. Rather than post a 20-character link that includes a lot of random words and numbers, you can instead create a bit.ly link that is shorter, more visually pleasing, and easier to fit into posts on platforms that have specific length requirements. Most short link tools also allow you to track the link's metrics to measure audience engagement with that particular link over time. Currently, there are almost 30 billion links that have been shortened using the bit.ly tool alone.

Platform-Specific Tips and Suggestions

Because platforms are constantly changing, I have included platform-specific tips and suggestions on the book's companion website (www.mypiobook.com), where you can also find tutorials and other guidance for many of the social media platforms discussed in the book, including Twitter, Facebook, Instagram, Pinterest, LinkedIn, Academia.edu, and ResearchGate.

9

BUILDING AND ENGAGING WITH ONLINE COMMUNITIES

Why Engage With Online Communities?

Throughout the chapters in this book, you may have encountered digital communities with which you want to join and engage. You may also have some ideas for online communities that you think are missing and that you want to develop yourself. There are lots of reasons why you might want to engage with or create an online community. There are also probably a lot of communities that you are already a member of. List some of the online communities (personal and professional) that you are already a member of here:

_____   _____

_____   _____

_____   _____

_____   _____

_____   _____

Reasons for Joining Online Communities

There are several reasons for joining online communities, but the following are some of the most popular reasons for academics and higher education professionals.

Sharing resources.
In many fields and disciplines, we do not want to re-create the wheel. If a resource already exists that would be helpful to our work, we try to seek it out. Online communities are great for learning about resources that you might not have been previously aware of, learning about new resources as they are developed, and sharing about your own resources that could help other people.

Building a network.

For new academics and higher education professionals, online communities are a great source for building relationships with colleagues across disciplines and all over the world. You never know where your network will come in handy, so nurturing relationships with colleagues, whether online or face-to-face, is always a smart investment of your time and energy.

Learning about a new field or discipline.

When you are just getting started in a new field or discipline, or if you decide to switch your field or discipline midcareer, online communities that are made up of a mix of peers and more senior colleagues become wonderful spaces to become acculturated to your new area. Online communities can help you learn the common language, customs, and nuances of your field or discipline.

Finding collaborators.

Throughout your career, you will find yourself in need of partners and collaborators on a range of projects. Online communities help you to expand your network so that you are aware of a lot more people in your field or discipline. The next time that you need to staff a committee for your national organization, find a coauthor for a book chapter, or locate resources for that new class you are designing, your online Rolodex may provide the collaborators you are seeking.

Becoming an influencer.

Frequent contributors to online communities can become influencers in their field or discipline. As long as the engagement is useful and genuine, online communities can help you to be heard and seen in a much broader way than your local institutional engagements and face-to-face conference participation might.

Having fun.

Online communities, although serious about engaging with their interest in a topic or issue, are also about having fun. Colleagues will often share jokes, memes, and funny stories about their professional lives in ways that create stronger bonds within the group and bring some levity to the discussions at hand. You will genuinely enjoy the people you are hanging out with online, so look for ways to insert fun into your communities as well.

Take a moment to think about other reasons why you might want to seek out additional online communities at this stage in your career and write them down here:

1. _____

2. _____

3. _____

4. _____

In addition to the benefits of online communities, there is a huge range of ways to find them, join them, and create them. In the first part of this chapter, I focus on strategies and tips for engaging in online communities that already exist. You will learn how to find communities that fit your interests and use proper digital etiquette in those communities. In the second half of this chapter, I will share some ideas for how to form communities online, including some of the typical platforms that will help you to connect with others online and form relationships around common interests, job responsibilities, or future career goals. I end the chapter by discussing ways to transition online relationships to offline encounters and collaborations.

Engaging in Already Existing Online Communities

There are many places to find online communities related to your field and discipline. The following are a few places that you might want to start looking to see what already exists for you to join and contribute to.

Listservs

Listservs are e-mail groups where people often post questions, share resources, and provide information about situations like job opportunities within a field or discipline. Many academic associations have their own listservs, and there are many listserv directories for finding the ones that might be of most interest to you (see Box 9.1 for some listserv directory examples). Joining a listserv is a great way to hear about the topics and issues that are of most interest in a particular field or discipline. By responding to questions and providing helpful resources to colleagues, listservs are also a great avenue for networking and building a strong reputation.

Academic and Disciplinary Associations

Many academic and disciplinary associations have a strong web presence, including a website, social media accounts, and an e-mail listserv. If you are already a member of an academic or disciplinary organization, check out its website to find opportunities to engage with other members. Some associations also host webinars, tweet chats, and other online community events that you can sign up to attend.

BOX 9.1.
Listserv directory examples.

- American Library Association (http://lists.ala.org/sympa)—specific to libraries
- H-Net (www.h-net.org/lists)—specific to the humanities and social sciences
- CataList (www.lsoft.com/catalist.html)—compendium of listserv groups searchable by topic

Alumni Groups

Colleges and universities are getting better and better about engaging their alumni online. To connect with other alumni from institutions where you earned your degree(s), check out the alumni pages on the institutions' websites to see if they are active on social media or whether they have created a list of alumni searchable by geographic location or company. Many colleges and universities have also created groups on various social media platforms (more on this in a moment). Although not an online community, many alumni offices also organize face-to-face meet-ups in cities around the country (this can depend on the size of the institution).

Social Media Groups

There are several social media platforms that have group functions where you can engage with colleagues through posting resources, communicating via discussion boards, and connecting in other ways. LinkedIn and Facebook are two of the more popular group-building platforms where you can create "pages" for a group or company, market those pages to people who might be interested in the topic or area of interest, and build a following of people who also contribute to the group. Finding these groups is relatively easy because the group creators usually want to grow their groups. Typically, you can just put some keywords into the platform's search bar and peruse the results.

Hashtags

Online communities can also converge around a particular hashtag. This is especially true on social media platforms such as Twitter. Group hashtags allow users to more easily organize tweet chats and exchange resources connected to a shared interest or topic area. (For more on popular hashtags in higher education see chapter 8.)

Bloggers

Finding and connecting with bloggers who are writing about your areas of interest is another way to form a community online. You will want to make sure to comment on blog posts so that the writer knows of your interest, and this can sometimes lead to interesting conversations, additional resources, and collaborations. If you are a blogger yourself, many comment functions allow you to enter your own web address when you post so that other bloggers and commenters can check out your blog as well. You can find other bloggers with similar interests to yours by using tools like Triberr (http://triberr.com).

Tips on Netiquette

If you are entering into any already existing communities, it is important to note that there may be cultural norms to which you will want to be attentive. The following are some of the main areas of online etiquette (or "netiquette") to be aware of.

Introduce yourself.
When you are new to an online community, it can be useful to let people know that you are there, what you are hoping to gain, and what you might be able to contribute to the conversation. This introduction does not have to be lengthy and you should first explore the online space to see if there is a specific area where these kinds of introductions are typically posted.

Be cautious about selling your own services.
Many online communities have explicit rules about promoting your own products and services. If you are joining an online community for this purpose, consider reaching out to the community's organizer(s) to ask about policies regarding self-promotion. Because online communities are about building genuine relationships and providing support, it is often seen as inappropriate and rude if someone joins solely to promote their products or services, no matter how useful they might be within the community.

Balance offering assistance and asking for it.
Online community is about relationship-building, so you want to make sure that your engagement in any community is a double-sided connection in which you are both giving and receiving the benefits of the community. This means that you will not want to depend on a community only to answer your questions and provide you resources; you should also think about the kinds of resources and information you can offer that will be helpful to others.

Be aware of previous discussions.
If you have been a member of an online community for any length of time, you have probably seen the same questions being asked over and over again. If you have a basic question to pose to the community, consider browsing the archives (many listservs have them) or scrolling through previous posts to see if the topic has already been covered. Online community members who are always asking questions that have already been addressed can quickly develop poor reputations among their colleagues. It is also considered poor form to ask questions that could be answered by a basic Google search.

Joining already existing online communities is a great way to build relationships online, find resources that can be helpful to your work, share experiences, and form new collaborations and partnerships.

Forming New Online Communities

Inevitably, you will develop a need for a community that does not already exist online and may want to create your own. Creating a community online can have varying levels of difficulty, depending on your goals for the community and how large you want the community to be. For example, Facebook as a whole is an online community that would be quite ambitious to emulate, but creating a Facebook group is a much more manageable task. Take a moment to write down any ideas you have for communities that you feel are missing from your professional life. You can also write down any online communities that exist but that are underdeveloped or struggling (see Box 9.2 for an example of one higher education professional who built an international online community).

_____

_____

_____

_____

_____

When you think about these online communities, what are the kinds of goals that you have for creating a community? Write down your top three goals:

1. _____

_____

2. _____

_____

3. _____

_____

Next, who do you think would benefit most from joining this community? Write down some of the characteristics of your ideal community members:

_____   _____

_____   _____

_____   _____

_____   _____

Ideas for Forming Community Online

Now that you have some basic ideas, there are several different ways that you can think about helping to shape and form a community online. In addition to the ideas mentioned previously such as listservs, associations, social media groups, hashtags, and blogs, you might want to consider the following:

BOX 9.2.
Virtually connecting at conferences.

Maha Bali
Associate professor of practice
Center for Learning and Teaching
The American University in Cairo

Blog: https://blog.mahabali.me
Twitter: https://twitter.com/Bali_Maha
Virtually Connecting: http://virtuallyconnecting.org
YouTube: www.youtube.com/VirtuallyConnecting

Living and working in Egypt, as a mother of a young child, Maha cannot always attend the academic conferences that are offered on the other side of the world. To stay connected with colleagues, Maha turned to digital tools, using virtual conference options to attend and tweeting with conference attendees she knew to experience conferences through others' sharing and feedback.

But, eventually, this was not enough; she was missing out on the social aspects of conferences that occur outside of the scheduled sessions. Moreover, Maha realized that other academics around the world were facing the same challenges, whether for social, financial, logistical, or health reasons. In 2015, Maha and her friend Rebecca Hogue piloted and later launched Virtually Connecting, a free service that provides opportunities for virtual participants to converse with people attending conferences face-to-face.

Virtually Connecting works by pairing an on-site buddy and a virtual buddy (volunteer members of the VC team) to schedule and facilitate conversations with on-site guest speakers and participants, so virtual participants can have a live video conversation with those present at the conference. These conversations are open to anyone to join, and they are also live-streamed and recorded for those who cannot join synchronously. Using over 100 Virtually Connecting volunteers, the group works with conferences to create a virtual experience that is open for everyone and helps to amplify the voices of those not able to participate in conferences face-to-face.

What started with two friends trying to connect with each other has grown tremendously in a short time. In 2016, Virtually Connecting offered 75 sessions at 20 events in 6 countries.

Choose a home base.
There are now several platforms that are available to help you to create a home base for your online community where members can create profiles, post resources, share ideas, contribute to discussion boards, and more (see Box 9.3 for some examples of these platforms). Your professional website can also serve as a possible home base as well (for more on this see chapter 7), especially if you are just looking to post information about the community although it typically meets and engages elsewhere (e.g., on a social media platform).

BOX 9.3.
Platforms for building online communities.

- CMNTY (www.cmnty.com)
- Mighty Networks (https://mightynetworks.com)
- Socibd (www.socibd.com)

Attend webinars.
Live online discussions and presentations through webinars can be a great way to find people who are also interested in the topics and issues that you are exploring. By offering a free webinar on a topic, you can create a space for people to congregate and then follow up with them to see who might be interested in additional conversation (see more about webinar platforms and resources in chapter 11).

Connect masterminds.
Mastermind groups are small communities of people who meet to share resources based on their career stage or interest in a particular topic. For example, I host a mastermind group related to academics who have side businesses in addition to our day jobs. Mastermind groups are perfect for online community because they can meet via phone or video chat. Ideally, these groups should have consistent meetings so that the online community becomes a resource for questions and troubleshooting as individual needs arise.

Curate resources.
There are several platforms for academics and higher education professionals to collect and curate resources that can then be shared with a group. Citation management systems often have group sharing settings as do social bookmarking sites. Creating and then publicizing groups that you create on these platforms can help you to find people who want to connect around your area or topic of interest.

Write collaboratively.
Group blogs or shared online publications through platforms such as Medium are other ways to find people who are interested in the topics and issues that you are passionate about. Although many of these already exist, it has never been easier to create a shared publication space and invite others to join and share ideas and resources together. Website plug-ins like Disqus (https://disqus.com/) can also help to manage user comments and strengthen community engagement around a blog-writing platform.

Share data.
Academics and higher education professionals also have many outlets to share their data. Resources such as the Open Science Data Cloud make it easier for researchers to share their own data and access the data of colleagues around the world. Although not all scholars will want to share their data sets, this serves as another possibility for forming online communities around specific research areas.

Foster discussion.

Platforms like Slack, a web- and app-based messaging system, and Proboard, a free hosting platform for discussion boards, can help users to cultivate conversations around particular topics and issues. Of course, these discussions can also happen in social media groups, via tweet chats, through blog commenting, and in a range of other mediums.

These are just a few of the ways that you can consider creating your own forms of community online. Knowing your goals for the community and who your ideal members would be is a strong starting point that will help you to choose the appropriate platform where your online community can thrive (see Box 9.4 for one example of a thriving online community).

Transitioning Online Relationships Offline

Although online relationships can be very rich, there may come a time where you want to meet your online colleagues in offline spaces. The following ideas can help you to transition your online relationships offline.

Conference Presentations

If there is someone in your field or discipline who would make a good conference copresenter, consider submitting a proposal together so that you can travel to the same conference at the same time.

Location-Based Meet-Ups

If you want to meet with your community members, but do not have a specific person in mind, let your community know where you are going to be when you are traveling for conferences or other events. This will allow you to schedule location-based meet-ups where you can go to a meal or otherwise meet in person with members of your online community.

Project-Based Meet-Ups

If your online community is engaging in a project together, such as working on a book, an event, or other large endeavor, consider scheduling a face-to-face retreat for everyone to gather in person. This kind of dedicated in-person meet-up can sometimes help a group to complete a project faster or more efficiently.

Campus Speaking Invitations

Consider inviting members of your online community to speak on your campus (or ask them to do the same for you) when appropriate. If you are in the same discipline or field, it can be helpful to have a member of your online community visit your campus to meet with you and various other colleagues so that you can learn from one another in person.

BOX 9.4.
Using social media to listen.

Cathy Hannabach
Editor, podcaster, and author

Find Cathy online:
Professional website: https://cathyhannabach.com
Ideas on Fire: http://ideasonfire.net
Imagine Otherwise podcast: http://ideasonfire.net/episodes
Twitter: https://twitter.com/channabach
LinkedIn: www.linkedin.com/in/cathyhannabach

At the heart of Cathy's online presence is experimentation. Because platforms can come and go, she appreciates that tools that work now might not work in the future. While Cathy engages in social media platforms to communicate and build community, she also works to create online spaces where she has more control, like her personal website.

Cathy has also chosen to use her social media presence to listen, learn about individuals' questions and problems, and point to resources that might provide solutions. Although social media is often seen as a tool for broadcasting information and promoting one's work and ideas, she is very aware that broadcasting can work both ways and that you can learn a lot by being attentive to online conversations and questions.

Listening to the conversations in her community led Cathy to launch Ideas on Fire, an academic publishing consultancy with services for academics who engage with issues of social justice, and to create the Imagine Otherwise podcast, where she interviews people working at the intersection of art, academia, and activism.

Based on her passions, Cathy has cultivated communities and built platforms where she can share her own and others' work in a way that aligns with her professional values and activist identity.

Help Other Community Members Meet Each Other

Even if you cannot attend a certain conference or event, your community members might be able to go. Use your online community to assist people in setting up meetings with one another to help strengthen the community overall.

Online community is an incredibly important component of professional digital identity. Hopefully, this chapter provided you with some ideas for where to find community, how to engage in already existing communities, and how to create online communities of your own if and when you need them.

RESPONDING TO
ONLINE CONFLICT

This chapter was probably the hardest one for me to write. As much as it pains me to say it, privilege is not blurred by the Internet; rather, it is amplified. It not only is troubling that academics are being targeted online for expressing their political views and/or sharing their scholarship but also clear that there are certain groups of academics who are being targeted more than others solely based on having one or more marginalized identities. A false sense of anonymity is certainly part of the problem—people may feel braver online when they can hide behind a depersonalized avatar or screen name—but it is also true that privilege is alive and well in many spaces, online and off.

It can be difficult to know what to do when one is the target of an attack online; it can be equally difficult to see colleagues being attacked and be unsure how to respond. This chapter will offer you some strategies for both situations. Although I deeply believe in the power of online communities to create positive spaces for academics, I am also a realist. I have seen how certain people are treated online and know this is a topic that cannot be ignored. Because I do not belong to all the marginalized groups that I will be mentioning in this chapter, I have reached out to colleagues to better understand their experiences with online conflict. (All names used in this chapter to describe the stories of academics I talked with have been changed to protect their privacy.) I have also compiled the small literature that exists on this topic to provide articles, blog posts, and other resources that might be useful to those concerned about, or currently experiencing, online conflict.

Forms of and Responses to Online Conflict

There are several different categories of people who may engage in conflict with academics and higher education professionals online. In this section, I outline the four most common groups. Throughout this chapter, I also provide examples of academics and higher education professionals who have encountered this type of behavior.

Trolls

Online trolls are people who go online primarily for the purpose of engaging in conflict. They are looking for particular kinds of topics, hashtags, and conversations so that they can intentionally and purposefully contribute hateful messages. Good examples of trolls are groups and organizations that seek out conversations on race to post messages about White supremacy. This was especially evident during the Charlottesville White supremacist march at the University of Virginia that occurred in August 2017. Trolls can be especially frustrating to encounter because they are not online to engage in dialogue but merely wish to poison conversations about topics with which they fundamentally disagree. Many interactions with trolls will be "drive-bys" where a troll will comment and move on, but other interactions can turn into bullying situations (more on this in a moment).

For this reason, the best response to trolls can be to not engage with them directly and block them from following your accounts. If an Internet troll threatens violence toward you, reporting the message(s) to the social media platform may result in their removal. If the threats of violence are personalized enough to make you fear for your safety, reporting the messages to your local police station and to your campus security is a must. Although this kind of action is rarely needed, it is recommended that you plan accordingly, especially if you have a politicized discipline, research project, or you post about topics related to politics, marginalized identities, or other issues that are magnets for trolls.

Haters

Haters may be less intentional about seeking out conflict on the Internet, but their comments can be just as biting as the trolls'. Comments by haters might include direct challenges to your scholarship or other work that are clearly uninformed, personal attacks, and just plain rude comments about your posts. In many cases, haters are people you do not know, but in some situations, they may be other people in your field or your institution you interact with at conferences or other campus meetings. Comments from haters are often sarcastic, and may be meant to be humorous, but cross a line.

Choosing how to respond to haters is best done on a case-by-case basis. If haters are unknown to you, ignoring their comments and blocking them from your account is completely appropriate. If a hater is known to you, you might decide to message the person privately to ask about the tone of the comment. In the case of one junior faculty member I advised who had a senior scholar in her field refer to a piece of her scholarship as "B.S." in a public online forum, I encouraged her to privately message the scholar, acknowledge the comment, and politely ask if that scholar had any specific feedback that might improve this junior scholar's future work. In this case, killing with kindness might be the best response to call attention to inappropriate behavior.

Bullies

Online bullying (also called *cyberbullying* or *cyberstalking*; see Hitchcock, 2017) occurs when a pattern of negative interaction happens over a period of time by the same person or the same group of people targeted at the same person or the same group of people when it has been requested that the behavior stop. In his book *So You've Been Publicly Shamed*, John Ronson (2015) discusses this phenomenon at length and describes it as a modern-day version of flogging in the public square. Academics can experience online bullying if they are public figures, if their work is politicized in any way (either inherently or is perceived to be so by others outside the academy), or if they are members of marginalized groups being targeted during specific national events, such as some of the negative online response by White supremacists to the ongoing Black Lives Matter campaign.

Online bullying is incredibly dispiriting, demotivating, and disheartening for people experiencing it and for those around them who are witnesses. It can cause depression and feelings of loneliness and isolation for those being targeted. Some scholars have quit social media platforms altogether after experiencing online bullying events (Flaherty, 2017b). Other scholars have called for institutions to have a systematic response for employees who experience bullying or threats online (Flaherty, 2017a).

If you experience online bullying, there are several possible responses: (a) block people who are bullying you; (b) if the bullying is extreme, take a social media break, delete your accounts, and come back with a fresh start; or (c) speak out against the bullies. Although this last option is certainly not for everyone—and should be done only if you feel it is safe to do so—calling out online bullies for their behavior can be an effective strategy to stop what most people can see is incredibly unprofessional behavior. If the bullying is occurring from a member of your own institution, reporting that bullying at your place of work is an additional possibility. (See Box 10.1 for additional information about responding to online conflict without the protection of tenure.)

Critics

Unlike trolls, haters, and bullies, critics may actually be engaging with your work. They may have negative things to say, but they are attempting (or are more open) to have a dialogue with you. These comments may be rude or sarcastic, or they may

BOX 10.1.
Encountering online conflict without the protection of tenure.

Many academics and higher education professionals may experience some form of online conflict without the protection of tenure. This can make possible responses more limited out of fear that any response could backfire and result in censure from one's institution or, at the very worst, being fired. This is a very real concern for administrators, contingent faculty, and other higher education professionals who are not in tenured positions (e.g., Flaherty, 2017c). Knowing your institution's policy for social media engagement, if it has one at all, is one way to protect yourself. If you encounter online conflict, discussing it with a department chair or other supervisor right away is another strategy to ensure that the right people are informed about what you are experiencing.

come in the form of questions. For example, a critic might ask, "Why didn't you include such-and-such a scholar in your analysis? Did you do any research at all?" The difference between critics and trolls, haters, or bullies is that you will be able to see that they have actually engaged with your work enough to offer a critique that might be meaningful or useful to you. Unlike the previous example of calling out another scholar's work as "B.S.," critics will offer commentary that, although perhaps hard to hear, might actually be something for you to consider.

Responding to critiques is also a judgment call. In most cases, I recommend thanking the critic publicly for the feedback ("Thanks so much for pointing that out—I'll take a look!"), but then following up via a private conversation so that the person's criticism is taken "offline" to a direct messaging conversation or via e-mail. In many cases, criticisms that I have received (and some were very helpful) actually came via private messages or e-mails to begin with. Many critics are aware that their negative or questioning comments about your work are for you alone and are not for public consumption.

Politicized Research, Scholarship, and Teaching

For academics whose work is already embedded with political meaning (e.g., scholars in women's and gender studies, ethnic studies, political science, climate studies, and many other fields), engaging online can be especially contentious territory. Because this work is already politicized by default, even sharing resources that will be of interest to disciplinary colleagues can be taken as a political statement even if it is not intended as such. Scholars in these fields may also be expected to respond to certain national or international events and be challenged by others in their disciplines if they remain silent (see Box 10.2 for one academic's story).

Strategies for Engaging in Online Spaces

Scholars from politicized disciplines have offered several suggestions for engaging in online spaces.

Find allies.
Seek out others in your field who are also engaging in discussions on your topic or area. Learn about the hashtags, private Facebook groups, and leaders in these areas whom you will want to follow and join. Once you have found a small group, feel free to ask for suggestions about who else they follow or where else they are engaging in online community.

Curate your feed.
You do not need to follow everyone who follows you, and I would recommend that you do not. Check out user profiles of the people who follow you before choosing to follow them back. On Twitter, for example, you can glance through the most recent tweets of a new follower to see if the posts might be of such interest to you that you would want to see them in your feed.

BOX 10.2.
It's hard to know how to do it right: Maria's story.

Maria, a junior faculty member at a small liberal arts college in the Northeast, struggles to know what to post online. As a woman of color who identifies as a feminist, she has been encouraged to post online and to engage in social media as a way to express her views. The responses she has received, however, have frequently been negative.

"I get scared as a junior faculty member and as a woman of color—if I put my political opinion on social media, it could affect me. But this is what I teach and research about."

For Maria, drawing the line between her personal and professional lives has been particularly difficult. Her choices about what to post, and what national and international stories to respond to, leave her conflicted.

Although she wants to be perceived as an ally, the constant conflict she is faced with is exhausting.

Post facts with citations.
If you can provide links to citations that support your ideas and arguments, it can head off trolls, haters, and bullies who might accuse you of stating opinion rather than fact. Although this will not always be the case, citing work that supports what you are saying is generally a helpful academic practice.

Share others' work.
An important part of being online is engaging with others' work and sharing out to your community what they could find interesting. By posting about the work of others in your field, you can create a broader context to talk about your own work and scholarship.

Post progress, not content.
If you feel the content you are researching is too sensitive to share, consider posting progress updates about your work without discussing the content. You can always share that you are working on an article, or prepping a new class, without disclosing the topic.

Share content via direct messaging.
Because many platforms have ways to engage in one-on-one conversations with other users, consider using this method, rather than a one-to-many post, to share your work with specific people who might find it interesting or useful. You can also share other people's content this way if you are concerned about posting it publicly.

Know conflict is coming.
Eventually, you will probably experience a troll, hater, bully, or critic, and knowing it is coming is half the battle. Part of the power of comments by people engaging

in online conflict is catching us off guard. For the most part, these critics will be strangers, so treat them accordingly. It can actually provide some comic relief to imagine some of the comments you will receive online being said to you face-to-face. (See Box 10.3 for one academic's experience responding to unexpected conflict.)

Do not engage.
Trolls, haters, and bullies, in particular, are goading you in the hope that you will engage with them and start a conflict that they can make public. By ignoring comments by these people, you can shut down most of the conflict from the very beginning. If you need to engage for some reason, try to do it privately as discussed previously in this chapter.

Ask for help.
If you are receiving unwanted negative attention online for something related to your professional life, contact your campus public affairs office. This office is trained to deal with unwanted attention and may be able to help you by vetting negative e-mails and social media posts, responding to media requests if the situation escalates, and generally advising you on how best to move forward following an online attack.

Block people when needed.
When you are experiencing inappropriate online conflict, it is not the time to be polite. Block people and report their behavior to the platforms where they are making

---

BOX 10.3.
Negative responses to public scholarship: Karen's story.

Several years ago, Karen was unprepared for the response she received for an op-ed piece she wrote for her local paper based on a recent book she had published.

The editorial, which included a sentence challenging the use of a particular word as too masculinized, had immediate negative response via online comments and e-mails to Karen.

Many of the negative comments attacked Karen as a woman. One comment called her a "feminist whiner" and questioned whether she should be a professor. Another suggested that she be fired.

Karen describes her reaction: "In our everyday lives, we expect pushback, but it's usually done in a polite fashion—the kind of language being used was out of my realm of experience." She chose to respond to many of the online comments, offering more attention to those who gave legitimate critiques.

Karen has found it helpful to remember that those leaving negative comments do not know her and that they are responding to the content rather than to her as a person. Despite the negative reactions she received, Karen believes it is her responsibility to bring work to the public, irrespective of the trolls she might encounter online.

comments. It is possible the trolls, haters, or bullies are breaking policies and can be forcibly removed from the platform.

Record negative communications.

If you are experiencing personal threats, slurs, or other forms of negative communications online, record the communications via screenshots or other methods so that you have a record of the event that you can share with your campus security or, if necessary, law enforcement.

As mentioned previously, extreme comments call for extreme measures. If you are ever concerned for your own or others' safety, report online comments to local authorities and your campus police. If needed, delete your account and take a break from online engagement for a while.

Witnessing Online Conflict

Even if you do not experience online conflict yourself, it is possible that you will witness it happening to someone you know or follow (see Box 10.4 for more about situations when online conflict is targeting students). There are several ways that you can express support to colleagues who are being targeted by trolls, haters, or bullies online.

Acknowledge the attack.

Although it may be more comfortable to ignore online conflict, it is important that you tell the target of the conflict that you see it happening and condemn it. Targets of online attacks can feel alone and are sometimes confused about why they are being attacked and whether it is warranted or justified. Even short messages of support can mean a lot.

Ask how you can help.

If you are not sure how you can help as a bystander to online conflict, privately message the target and ask what he or she needs or wants you to do. Whether the target is engaging in a coordinated counterattack or just asking for moral support from colleagues, it is best to go to the source.

BOX 10.4.

Witnessing online conflict among students.

Unfortunately, our students can also become targets of online conflict as junior scholars, as active citizens of their campus political events, because of a marginalized identity, or for a range of other reasons. If you see a student being attacked by trolls, haters, or bullies, you can use some of the strategies discussed in this chapter to offer your support. Additionally, you may want to report the conflict to your student affairs office or campus security so that they can reach out to the student with additional resources and guidance.

Unfollow trolls, haters, and bullies.
When people you follow engage in inappropriate online conflict, unfollow them. In other words, do not give them an audience. You can also take the extra step of privately messaging or e-mailing them to explain what caused you to unfollow if you know them and feel your feedback would make a difference.

Report trolls, haters, and bullies.
Do not expect that the target of online conflict will have reported the trolls, haters, or bullies who are attacking. Even if the the behavior has been reported, it can strengthen the report if others also share that they found the comments to be inappropriate. Reporting the person to the platform where the inappropriate behavior is occurring and to his or her university (when applicable) are both possibilities.

Express public support.
If the person being attacked, or someone in an ally group, has created a hashtag to demonstrate support, use it. You can also post about the situation, why you are supporting this colleague, and ask others in your online communities to also lend their support to the situation.

Online conflict, just like face-to-face conflict, is an extremely unfortunate part of academic discourse. Although this chapter provides some resources for how to respond when you or colleagues experience online attacks, how you choose to engage is a personal decision that will often have to be made in the moment on a case-by-case basis. For a growing library of resources on this topic, visit the book's companion website at www.mypiobook.com, where you can also suggest additional resources that should be included there.

Institutional Responses to Online Conflict Against Employees

Institutions may also struggle to know how to respond when one of their employees or students is targeted in an online conflict. (See Box 10.5 for one academic's experience receiving assistance from an institution in response to an online attack.) Ferber (2017) offers 12 helpful suggestions for institutions regarding how to respond to online conflict:

1. Be prepared with a protocol in place. Be proactive, not reactive.
2. Put safety first.
3. Universities should publicly condemn the form of the attack itself. Universities must support civil dialogue, and name abuse and harassment for what it is.
4. Provide faculty members with resources (who to call for help of various kinds) and information about what they may experience next.
5. Some people want to be kept in the loop and know what is going on, others don't—honor that.
6. Provide someone to review e-mails (preferably someone in public safety who can recognize threats more easily) so the attacked faculty member does not have

BOX 10.5.

Seeking support in responding to online conflict: Jack's story.

When he was the target of online trolls after a story about the campus unit he directs was picked up by *Breitbart*, Jack was immediately contacted by the public relations office of his institution, which offered support in managing the incoming media requests.

Jack received over 100 e-mails and innumerable social media engagements from alt-right and White supremacist individuals who disagreed with the story that had been picked up by various alt-right blogs and shared around the Internet.

Although Jack eventually handed off most of his incoming e-mails to the public affairs office to review, initially he was vetting these messages himself. His advice? "If they sent me something that was aggressive or called me a name, I blocked them, and I recorded it."

The e-mails and social media messages ended about two weeks after the story died down, but Jack learned powerful lessons. "Know your resources and have backup." Not having to go through the situation alone, and having the support of his institution, was a key component of Jack's ability to get through the experience.

to. (Consider providing two different people, because just reading hundreds of e-mails of this type is disturbing).

7. Have presence of public safety in face-to-face classrooms where an attack has occurred, and offer faculty an escort on campus.

8. Ask faculty members what they need. Provide psychological services to faculty under attack.

9. Respect faculty members' desires for modification of future teaching responsibilities.

10. Treat the crises as immediate but also ongoing. The impact on faculty does not end after the fire is put out.

11. Do not individualize the problem. See these attacks as coordinated and planned. This is a systemic and cultural problem. Administrators across the nation should be discussing how to both prevent and deal with these incidents. They are not going to stop.

12. Learn from organizations with more experience in facing these challenges, such as the: Southern Poverty Law Center, Planned Parenthood, Institute for Research and Education on Human Rights, etc. Part of Planned Parenthood's goal is to respond with "Care and Compassion." This is something universities can learn from. (pp. 41–42)

No matter what your position, being targeted by an online attack, or witnessing one happening to someone else, can be unsettling and scary. Hopefully the suggestions in this chapter offer a starting point for possible responses when you are a target of or a witness to online conflict. The most important thing to remember is that you do not have to face the conflict alone. There are people and resources available to support you.

II

STRATEGIES TO CREATE
AND SHARE CONTENT WITH
LARGER AUDIENCES

According to Hoffman and Casnocha (2012), "all humans are entrepreneurs" (p. 3), but unless you have earned an MBA, you may not know exactly how to be entrepreneurial as an academic or higher education professional. Many of us have not really been taught how to promote our own work, how to share about our projects, or even how to embrace the creative parts of our academic lives. If you have found your way to this chapter, you may have a bit of an entrepreneurial spirit or at least a strong desire to share your work with a broader audience than you currently have. There are a range of ways that you might choose to regularly communicate with the people that you want to attract to your work, including enhancing your professional brand, creating products (including publications), advertising services, or just more broadly sharing your ideas. Throughout this chapter, I describe several possibilities and the basic components required to get started with each one. (For additional resources on sharing your work with broader audiences, see also Carrigan, 2016; Gasman, 2016; and Tyson, 2010.)

E-Mail Lists and Newsletters

Many people think that e-mail lists are *the* best way to connect with an audience. The e-mail inbox is considered by some to be a sacred space because it is a medium through which you have someone's undivided attention—that is, if he or she chooses to open and read the e-mails that you send. It is true that e-mail inboxes can be less noisy than other social media platforms, and if you have been invited into that space by someone who is interested in your work and projects, she or he may be more likely to read whatever it is that you are sending there.

If you are considering starting an e-mail list, it can be helpful to begin by looking at the e-mail lists that you currently belong to and ask yourself the following:

- What made me want to join those lists?
- Where did I find out about the lists that I have joined?
- Do the creators of those lists offer me anything special for joining them?
- Do I read all the e-mails that I receive from the lists I have joined? Why or why not?
- How frequently am I receiving e-mails from the lists that I have joined?
- Are there any e-mail lists from which I have unsubscribed? Why did I unsubscribe?

Your answers to these questions can help you decide the kinds of content that you might want to create for an e-mail list, the frequency with which you will send those e-mails, and where you will market your e-mail list so that people can join your list and sign up to hear from you.

Initial Steps

Once you have decided to create an e-mail list, you will need a few things.

A place for people to sign up for the list.

When building an e-mail list, best practice necessitates that you allow people to sign up for the list voluntarily rather than creating a list and adding people to it yourself. This means that you will need to have a "home base" where people can find information about the list, sign up to receive your e-mails, and maybe even see examples of what you have sent to your list in the past (a professional website is a good choice for this; you can read more about creating a professional website in chapter 7).

A way to e-mail the people on your list.

Once you start building your e-mail list, you will want to have a way to easily e-mail the people who sign up using professional-looking e-mail templates. There are several services that can assist with this (see Box 11.1 for more information) and that can help you create automated sign-ups, schedule out e-mails in advance, and provide helpful

BOX 11.1.
E-mail service providers.

E-mail service providers like MailChimp, Constant Contact, GetResponse, or ConvertKit can help you manage e-mail lists and send out professional-looking e-mails using standardized templates. These providers often have advanced features (some for an increased fee) where you can create automated response e-mails, automated e-mail campaigns, or subgroups based on your list members' interests, among many other options. Some providers are free for a certain list size, but they may not include the more advanced features described here. If you are serious about building an e-mail list, an e-mail service provider is worth considering.

templates for e-mail design. WiseStamp (http://wisestamp.com) is another tool that can help you to create professional-looking and promotional e-mail signatures.

A reason for the list.
It will be hard to convince people to sign up for your e-mail list if they do not know what the list is for or if they do not think that they will benefit from it. Thus, it is helpful for you to have a clear idea of the goal of your list and to clearly communicate that goal to potential subscribers. The following list highlights some potential e-mail list goals:

- To help keep people up-to-date with your current projects
- To e-mail regular blog posts out to your followers
- To sell products or services
- To provide information on a particular topic or area (i.e., establish your expertise)
- A combination of these options

I keep a couple of lists that have different goals. One list is for professional and personal contacts who want to receive monthly e-mails about my projects (e.g., my blog posts, books, and podcasts). The second list is for people who want to receive a weekly essay that I write. Both lists are an opt-in sign-up on my professional website. The content of the second e-mail is also publicly posted on the blog of my professional website so that people can access the essays there if they do not want to join the list.

Once you have a reason for your list, you will want to stick to it. If people sign up for your list to receive your blog posts but then you switch goals and try to sell them something, it may cause them to unsubscribe. You want to be honest with your list subscribers about what they will get when they sign up, which means openly sharing the purpose of your list and the planned frequency of your e-mails with subscribers.

A welcome message.
Once people have joined your list, you want to make sure to welcome them with a thank-you message. This message can include a reminder about the frequency of e-mails they will be receiving, information on where to find out more about you, and your contact information. (See Box 11.2 for a sample welcome message from my own e-mail list.)

Maintenance

There are additional best practices to consider once you have started your e-mail list.

Be consistent.
If you say that you will send out weekly e-mails, then send weekly e-mails. If you do not think you can keep up with that schedule, then start with something less

BOX 11.2.
Sample e-mail list welcome message.

Welcome to "The Academic Creative" weekly newsletter!

Each week, I write an essay about topics like productivity, resilience, and what it means to learn like it's your job. Now this essay will come right to your e-mail inbox! You'll receive your first essay within the next seven days.

As a thank you for signing up, I hope you'll enjoy these three free productivity tools:

- Daily Goal Annual Tracker
- Daily To Do List
- Daily Done List

Please take a moment to hit "reply" to this e-mail, introduce yourself, and let me know the biggest question or challenge you have regarding your professional development right now. I love connecting with readers and shaping this newsletter to meet your needs. You can also connect with me on Twitter at twitter.com/@Katie__Linder.

I'm excited to share these essays with you each week—thanks again for inviting me into your inbox.

Happy reading!

---

frequent, like monthly e-mails, and increase later on if you need to. I send out my weekly e-mails at the same time every week (6 a.m. on Friday mornings) so that my readers know exactly when it will come to their inbox.

Be polite.
Someone has invited you into his or her inbox because he or she wants to hear more from you and that is quite an honor. Be respectful of the space by not writing outside of what you have previously promised, by not writing something that is overly long, and by not sharing the e-mail addresses you have collected with anyone else.

Be concise.
Think about how you typically read e-mails and the e-mail lengths that you prefer. In all likelihood, readers will be skimming your content, so be brief, to the point, and use numerical and bulleted lists where appropriate.

Be patient.
Building a strong (and large) e-mail list takes time. It requires that you tell people about the list (or make it easy to find), that you provide useful or interesting content on a regular basis, and that you do not give up on the list too soon if you are not

BOX 11.3.
Building an audience.

Bonni Stachowiak
Director of teaching excellence and digital pedagogy
Associate professor of business and management
Vanguard University
Host, *Teaching in Higher Ed* podcast

Find Bonni online:
Professional website: http://teachinginhighered.com
Twitter: https://twitter.com/bonni208
Google+: https://plus.google.com/+BonniStachowiak
Facebook: www.facebook.com/teachinginhighered
LinkedIn: www.linkedin.com/in/bonnistachowiak

In June 2014, Bonni launched the *Teaching in Higher Ed* podcast with the goal of building a community of practitioners who were passionate about teaching college students. Since then, she has cultivated an audience of thousands of listeners, many of whom also subscribe to her regular e-mail newsletter.

Over time, Bonni has grown her audience through consistent posting and quality content. She considers knowing your audience to be one of the most important components of building trust. Bonni's newsletter and podcast also allow her to nurture an online space of her own where she does not have to rely on other platforms (e.g., social media) to cultivate and connect with an audience.

Although she admits that being online involves taking risk, because anytime you share content you invite criticism, Bonni also says that thinking of podcasting as an act of service helps to keep her from being nervous about how others might perceive her as she shares through the *Teaching in Higher Ed* podcast and blog.

seeing the returns that you want. (See Box 11.3 for one higher education professional's experience with building an audience.)

If you decide to create an e-mail list, you should consider it a long-term investment. Although your goals for the list may change over time (and you can share that with your readers when it happens), the idea of building an audience through an e-mail list is an intentional commitment of your time, creativity, and other resources.

Blogging

Blogging is another excellent way to connect with people who want to hear from you on a regular basis, especially if you are interested in writing longer-form essays that do not fit within the typical length requirements of an e-mail or social media platform. A blog (short for *weblog*) is a place online where you post regular content for others to read. This content can be strictly professional in nature, a combination of professional and personal, or completely personal, depending on the content that you want to write.

Initial Steps

If you decide that you want to begin blogging, there are some basic components that you will need to get started.

A name.

Most blogs have a name so that they are easy to talk about and share with others. You will want to choose a name that is somewhat connected to the content that you are producing, but you can also get creative. For example, the collection of essays that I publish as blog posts is part of a newsletter that I send out each week called *The Academic Creative*. Some people prefer to include their full name in the blog title so that it is easy to find through a web search.

A web address.

If you are posting regular content to the web, you will need a place for it to reside. One option is a professional website (see more about this in chapter 7), or you can create a website that just houses your blog through a free service like WordPress, Tumblr, or Blogger. A third option is to post your content to a group blogging platform like Medium, so that others can find your posts and they are searchable within a larger body of other people's writing.

A blogging schedule.

You will also need to decide how frequently you would like to be posting to your blog. Although weekly (or more frequent) posts may drive more traffic to your blog, it can be challenging to keep up with that schedule if you struggle with ideas for what to write or if you cannot commit that amount of time to writing regularly. A consistent schedule is ideal, so choose whether you want to post weekly, twice per month, monthly, or otherwise before you get started. It is also a good idea to have a list of post topics in case you fall behind on your schedule and need a post idea. Use the space provided to note some ideas for potential blog posts that you might like to write:

1. _____

2. _____

3. _____

4. _____

5. _____

6. _____

7. _____

8. _____

A way for people to subscribe.
Most blog platforms allow subscribers to automatically receive your new content in two main ways: RSS feed and e-mail. RSS (or real simple syndication) is a way for people to receive your blog posts via a "feed reader" (examples include Feedly, Digg Reader, and The Old Reader). Feed readers are web- or app-based platforms that are notified when a new blog post or other web content that the user subscribes to becomes available. That available content is then collected into one space for ease of viewing. For those who do not have a feed reader, or who want to receive blog posts in multiple ways, e-mail subscription is another option. Your blog readers can sign up on your site by inputting their e-mail to then receive your blog posts directly into their inboxes. The e-mail service providers described in Box 11.1 usually include a way to embed a sign-up form within your website, so you can look for that feature when choosing a platform.

A way for people to share.
If people like your content, they will want to share it with others. Embedding social media share buttons on your blog can help your readers share what you are posting more easily. Using tools like ClickToTweet, you can also create links within your blog posts that add predrafted content to a Twitter status box when someone clicks on the link—you cannot make sharing easier than that!

Maintenance

There are some additional best practices to consider after you begin blogging.

Create quality content.
Although blogs can often be more informal, you will still want to make your blog worth reading, which means making sure that you spell and grammar-check all posts, include correct links and references, and produce content that other people will find interesting. When deciding what content to post, consider the kinds of blogs that you like to read. What draws your attention and keeps you committed to reading that author's posts?

Find good images.
When blog posts are linked online, particularly on social media platforms, they will be more likely to draw attention if they have an image associated with them. This is particularly true of text-based platforms like Twitter, where images can serve to break up a longer feed of only text-based updates. (See Box 11.4 for ideas on where to find images that you can use for your blog posts.)

BOX 11.4.
Image sources for blog posts.

- Everystockphoto: www.everystockphoto.com (use advanced search to find Creative Commons–licensed images that are free to use)
- Flickr: www.flickr.com
- Flickr Creative Commons: www.flickr.com/creativecommons (a way to search for Creative Commons–licensed images that are free to use)
- Fotolia: https://us.fotolia.com
- iStockPhoto: www.istockphoto.com
- NIH Photo Galleries: http://www.nih.gov/about/nihphotos.htm
- Stocksy: www.stocksy.com
- The Noun Project: https://thenounproject.com
- Wikimedia Commons: https://commons.wikipedia.org

Podcasting

Since I started podcasting in April 2015, it has become one of my favorite communication media. Podcasts are audio content (sometimes also including video) that can be shared via web players or smartphone apps. There are podcast shows for almost every topic you might think of and I currently host three podcasts: *Research in Action*, an interview-based show on topics and issues related to research in higher education with guests from a range of disciplines that I produce as part of my work as the Oregon State University Ecampus research director; *You've Got This*, a solo show for higher education professionals looking to increase their confidence and capacity for juggling the day-to-day demands of an academic life that I produce on the side out of my home; and *The Anatomy of a Book*, a solo podcast chronicling the writing of the book that you now hold in your hands and that I also produce out of my home. Additionally, I cohost an academic entrepreneurship and small business podcast called AcademiGig. (All the shows are linked from my professional website at www .katielinder.work if you want to check them out to.).

Initial Steps

If you think that podcasting might be interesting to try, there are some basics you need to know to get started.

You will need a way to record audio.

Most computers now come with a built-in microphone that you can use to record audio, but the sound quality might not be optimal. Well-produced podcasts pay attention to sound quality, and hosts will often have a special microphone and podcasting space that has sound-dampening foam or blankets. For the podcast I produce at Oregon State University Ecampus, we use a studio. For the podcast I produce at home, I record in a small closet lined with noise-reducing foam tiles.

In addition to the recording equipment, you will need a program on your computer to capture the audio that you are producing. Common audio production software that comes with most computers includes QuickTime (PC and Mac), Audacity (PC and Mac), and GarageBand (Mac). This audio recording software will allow you to capture your sound and provide tools for any audio editing that you will need to do. You can also use software products like Pamela, Call Recorder, or Audio Hijack to record audio if you are interviewing someone else via Skype or Google Hangout.

You will need a way to share your audio.
There are several fee-based platforms available to help you host and share the audio content that you create for your podcast (a few examples are Libsyn, SoundCloud, and Blubrry). These platforms help you to create an RSS feed (similar to the feed discussed with blog posting) that can be sent out to a range of platforms, including iTunes, SoundCloud, Stitcher, Google play, and other places where your audience may want to find and listen to your podcast. Expect to pay between $10 and $20 per month to host your podcast audio. New social media tools like Wavve (www .getwavve.com) can also help you to share short audio clips via platforms like Twitter, Instagram, and Facebook.

You will need a web presence for your podcast.
Most podcasts have their own websites so that alongside each audio episode you can share "show notes" that include links or references for the content that you mention on the show. Your podcast website might also include information about where to download the show, additional information about you as the host, and contact information in case listeners want to get in touch with you. If your podcast has sponsors, your website might also include information about them as well (see Box 11.5 for more information on monetizing a podcast).

BOX 11.5.
Monetizing a podcast.

If you want to start a podcast to make money, that is probably not the best goal to motivate you. Although podcasts can be monetized through sponsorships, it can be challenging to do this unless you have a large listener base. Most sponsorship packages will require thousands of downloads per episode, which may not be possible if you have a niche topic. That said, if you can find a sponsor that is directly tied to your topic and that your listeners will want to support, you can approach them to see if they are willing to sponsor your show. Typical sponsorships include a short ad included in each episode, with the sponsor offering something for your show's listeners (e.g., a discount code). It is common for sponsors to pay for this ad on a per episode, per week, or per month basis.

You will need a brand identity.
If you are producing a regular podcast, your show will need, at minimum, a name and some cover art (like a logo) that will be showcased on iTunes and other platforms. Think carefully about your podcast's name and brand because it can be hard to rebrand once you have a strong listener base.

You will need a topic.
Perhaps the most important requirement for your podcast is a topic. What is it that you think people will most want to hear about from you? What are you an expert in that people could benefit from learning more about? Podcast shows can be very niche, which is perfect for academic and higher education audiences. You will want to choose an area that can be explored from a range of angles and a topic where you feel that you have a lot of useful content to contribute to the overall conversation. Define your area of expertise and use that as the basis for your show.

Maintenance

There are some additional best practices to consider as you begin podcasting.

Be consistent.
Like blogging, podcasting works best in terms of building an audience and platform when you are producing regular content. *Research in Action* is a weekly show that posts every Monday. *You've Got This* posts twice-weekly episodes on Wednesdays and Saturdays. *The Anatomy of a Book* is released every Thursday. Whatever schedule you choose, make sure that you can stick to it. It is easier to increase your number of episodes than to decrease those episodes once you have a regular following of listeners.

Be passionate.
Even if your podcast topic is incredibly niche, there is a reason that you are interested in that area and you should share that passion with your listeners. In other words, embrace your topic—your enthusiasm will help your listeners care about your show, and you as an expert, all the more.

Connect with your audience.
Creating channels for your listeners to engage with you is very important. Social media can play an important role here, but you can also just provide your listeners with an e-mail address where they can offer feedback about the show. For all of my podcasts, I am most active promoting the shows and talking with listeners on Twitter, using the handles @RIA_podcast and @YGT_podcast in addition to my personal Twitter handle of @Katie__Linder.

Learn from others.
As you produce your own podcast, take time to listen to other shows and learn from them. What do you find particularly engaging or interesting about other

shows? What techniques do the hosts use that you find especially useful? How do other shows organize their show notes or websites in helpful ways that you might want to emulate? Always look for ways that you can make your podcast better for your listener audience. Also, there are several podcasting groups on Facebook that share advice and ideas (e.g., She Podcasts and Podcast Community), so you can also seek out online communities when you are getting started to learn more about additional resources (for more on engaging in online communities, see chapter 9).

Webinars

Webinars are an excellent way to connect with an audience when you want to provide extended content that does not work well in a text-based format, when you want to encourage live interaction with audience members, or when you just want to create an audience engagement medium where people can see you on live or recorded video. Many webinar platforms (see Box 11.6 for some examples) offer features to share video, share your screen, share a chat feature during the presentation, or share documents that can be downloaded by participants. Some will also offer accessibility accommodations such as a space to provide live captioning. Many platforms also offer the option to have more than one person as a presenter, so if you are planning to share a conversation between two people or a panel of speakers, you will want to make sure the webinar platform you choose supports that option.

Initial Steps

There are some basics of what you need to know to get started with webinars.

You will need a webcam.
If you plan to record yourself on video for the webinar, you will need a camera either that is built into your computer (this is standard with many desktop and laptop computers) or that you purchase and install.

BOX 11.6.
Webinar platforms.

- Adobe Connect: www.adobe.com/products/adobeconnect.html
- ClickMeeting: clickmeeting.com
- Crowdcast: www.crowdcast.io
- Google Hangout: hangouts.google.com
- GoToWebinar: www.gotomeeting.com/webinar
- WebEx: www.webex.com
- Zoom: https://zoom.us

You will need a strong Internet connection.

Because you will be using video, you will want to make sure that your Internet connection is strong enough to broadcast your video at a level of quality that will not distract attendees who come to the webinar. In some cases, this will mean that you use a hardwired Internet connection rather than wireless.

You will need a webinar platform.

To share your content with an audience, you will need to choose a webinar platform. There are a range of different platforms available that offer slightly different features. When I recently offered webinars to help promote my second book, I chose Crowdcast for ease of use, its audience engagement features, and because I like the look of its platform design. Now that I produce regular monthly webinars, I have invested in a platform called ClickMeeting that offers more features. Look through a range of platforms, explore their features, read online reviews, and try to view a recorded webinar on that platform before you make your choice.

You will need a way to e-mail attendees.

Before your webinar begins, you will want to remind participants to attend. After the webinar is over, you may want to follow up with attendees to provide additional information. The e-mail clients mentioned earlier in the chapter can help with this, but your webinar platform may also include this feature (although it may require that you pay a fee).

You will need a quiet space.

At the appointed time for your webinar to begin, you will want to make sure that you have a quiet space to record so that you and your attendees are not distracted by background noise or activity. If possible, make sure that children, pets, and roommates or partners are quiet as you record. Turn off the ringer on your cell phone if it will be in the same room with you and turn off any computer alerts (e.g., your e-mail) that could ding or beep in the middle of your recording.

You may need a "home base" to house information about the webinar.

Even if you are mostly planning to market your webinar via social media, it will be helpful if your webinar has a stable web presence, even if it is just a form for people to sign up to attend (see Box 11.7 for ideas for setting up web forms). Webinars work best if they are prescheduled and advertised so that you make sure they are reaching the right audience, but you can also offer a replay option for your webinar in case people miss the live viewing. A home base serves as one option to store this replay for future viewers, but you can also post it to an online platform like YouTube and then share the link via social media platforms (for one example of a webinar home base, see the website for my webinar series at www.howtoacademia .com).

BOX 11.7.
Web form options.

- Typeform: www.typeform.com
- WuFoo: www.wufoo.com

Maintenance

There are some additional best practices to consider as you begin producing webinars.

Practice.

If you are using a new webinar platform, or even if you are experienced with the webinar platform you have chosen, make sure to practice at least once before the live webinar to troubleshoot any issues that might arise. In one case, I learned through practicing that my webinar platform preferred one browser over another—troubleshooting that problem was not something I would have wanted to deal with five minutes before the live presentation. If you are planning to use presentation slides or other media with your webinar, include the transitions to these different elements in your practice session as well to make sure everything will run smoothly once the webinar is live.

Create an outline.

In the same way that you might prepare for a lecture or conference presentation, create a rough outline of what you plan to cover in your webinar so that you can stay on track and maintain your planned timing. Keep in mind that an outline is not the same thing as a script; you will not want to read directly from your notes during the webinar.

Use interesting visuals.

If you plan to share visuals other than a video of yourself, make them unique and interesting for your viewers. Tools like Canva and SlidesCarnival have presentation templates that can help those of us who are less experienced with creating impactful visual presentations.

Respect attendees' time.

The attendees for your webinar have signed up because they want to hear what you have to say, but you should still be respectful of their time and offer the information you are providing as concisely as possible. Webinars that run about 30 minutes are usually long enough to share what you want to say and provide time for a question-and-answer session. The longer the webinar recording, the less likely people are to watch the replay (and that may be where you get the greatest number of people engaging with the webinar).

Even if only a few people sign up to attend your webinar—or no one attends at all—the show must go on. Treat a small (or nonexistent) audience the same as you would a larger audience because you may get more people engaging with your webinar as a replay option once it has been recorded. Just as you watch television on demand, people will also choose to watch your webinar recording when it is most convenient for them.

Follow up.

After your webinar is over, e-mail all of the attendees (and the people who signed up but never showed) to share the link to the webinar replay and any resources that might be of use to the webinar audience. Try to send this e-mail out immediately following the webinar or as soon as the replay becomes available. (See Box 11.8 for one academic entrepreneur who is hosting a regular online conference using webinar presentations.)

Recorded or Live Videos

There are now several different platforms available for sharing live or recorded videos with a range of audiences. YouTube is probably the most popular video repository where you can create a "channel" and upload videos that can then be shared with a link or embedded into other websites. In fact, when writing this book, I created videos of a 10-day writing retreat I took in December 2016 and a 30-day writing challenge in April 2017 and posted them to my YouTube channel so that people could follow along with the book's progress. (Intrigued? Visit www .mypiobook.com for links to these videos.) Recorded videos are a great medium if you want to have a little more control over the production quality, because you have more opportunities for editing and for multiple recording sessions to get the video just right.

Live video sharing, which is now available via Google; Facebook Live; and apps like Periscope, Snapchat, and Instagram, is a more informal medium where it is more common to share shorter day-in-the-life clips, tutorials, or promotional clips for a product or service. Live video begins with the click of a button and then you are broadcasting on whatever platform you have chosen to use. Facebook Live, Periscope, and Google videos can be recorded and saved for future viewings, but Snapchat and Instagram videos are only available for less than a minute to up to 24 hours. Perhaps not too surprisingly, the more consistently you engage in both prerecorded and live video production, the greater the number of followers you have the potential to gain.

Initial Steps

The following are some basics you need to know to get started.

You will need a webcam, tablet, or smartphone.

When recording videos, you have the option of using a range of tools depending on the level of video quality that you want to produce. If you want high video quality,

BOX 11.8.
Hosting an online conference.

Jennifer Polk
Life coach and academic entrepreneur

Find Jennifer online:
Professional website: http://fromphdtolife.com
Self-employed PhD: http://selfemployedphd.com
Beyond the Professoriate: https://beyondprof.com
Twitter: https://twitter.com/FromPhDtoLife
Facebook: www.facebook.com/FromPhDToLife
LinkedIn: www.linkedin.com/in/jennifer-polk-bab56443/

When Jen graduated with her PhD in 2012, she wasn't sure she wanted a typical academic job. She created a blog, *From PhD to Life*, to share about her personal journey post–graduate school and began to connect with other PhDs who were not pursuing tenure-track positions. Jen used social media as a form of self-care during a time when she was geographically isolated from other academics experiencing what it means to choose a different career path.

Jen's platform of choice has been Twitter, where she uses hashtags such as #altac and #withaPhD to host "chats" and build relationships with colleagues and clients. Since her graduation in 2012, she has only worked for herself and has not been traditionally employed—in part because of the use of social media to grow her coaching and speaking business.

Jen's online community has also informed a current side business, Self-Employed PhD, where she facilitates a community of alternative academics who want to learn from one another's experiences as business owners who also have PhDs. With a colleague, she also launched an annual online conference called Beyond the Professoriate with the intention of connecting like-minded alternative academics.

As Jen continues to experiment and grow her coaching and entrepreneurial endeavors, her online presence now plays a central role in building and strengthening relationships with academics all over the world.

you should definitely use the webcam that comes installed on your desktop or laptop computer, or a separate webcam that you purchase for this purpose. Higher quality videos are mostly of the prerecorded variety. For live videos, tablet or smartphone quality is more appropriate, but keep in mind that tablets and smartphones are designed for convenience and not for high-quality video production.

You will need file storage space and bandwidth.
For prerecorded videos, it will be important to have a decent amount of file storage (at least a terabyte of space), especially if you plan to produce them regularly. For

example, a short five-minute video of high quality (720p) can require 500 MB; several of these videos will quickly take up your storage space. Less storage space will be needed if you plan to host your videos using cloud storage like a YouTube channel and not keep copies on your local drive.

For live video created with a tablet or smartphone, bandwidth will be more important than storage, but keep in mind that size of storage on your phone or tablet can also impact the amount of video that you can produce. You will probably not want to keep large amounts of video files on any mobile device. Live video production will be best when using a Wi-Fi network and will have poorer quality if created when connected to a cellular network, so you may want to record live videos when you have Wi-Fi available.

You may need editing software.
Depending on the kinds of videos that you want to produce, you may want to employ video editing software like Adobe Premier (PC) or iMovie (Mac), which can help you to add music, credit slides, and other elements to make your prerecorded videos appear to be more professionally produced. Apps like Snapchat and Instagram offer a range of filters and add-ons that you can use to modify your live videos, so no editing software is necessary for those.

You will need a platform to share your videos.
The platform where you choose to share your videos will depend on the kinds of videos you create and your intended audience. For prerecorded videos, YouTube is one of the most popular platforms for sharing videos with large and diverse audiences. YouTube allows you to upload a video, create a short description, tag your video to make it easier for people to find, and track viewing rates. For live videos, Facebook, Periscope, Snapchat, and Instagram are all popular options, but keep in mind that some platforms allow your videos to be recorded whereas others only show them for a brief period of time before they are gone forever.

Maintenance

There are some additional best practices to consider as you begin producing videos.

Practice on one platform at a time.
If you are just getting started with producing prerecorded or live video, choose one platform and get comfortable with it before branching out to other platforms. Although many video production and sharing platforms have different features, learning on one will give you a basic understanding of how to use others. Also, the more you practice, the more comfortable you will feel in front of the camera.

Be aware of your surroundings.
Get in the habit of taking a practice shot of yourself and reviewing what it looks like in terms of lighting, audio quality, and what is appearing behind you to ensure that

your video does not include anything in the background that you do not want your viewers to see. At the very least, you will want to review an entire video clip before you post it online to make sure that the quality, message, and content are what you intended.

Aim for quality, but not perfection.
People who watch your videos know that you are human and that you might make mistakes. Do not worry too much about creating a perfect video, but do decide what level of quality you are most comfortable with in terms of your own production skills and what you are willing to share with others.

Social Media Images

Once you are creating regular content, you will want to share about that content on social media platforms so that people can find what you are producing. Social media images, which can include pictures, graphics, and small animations, are an excellent way to share information. There are now several online tools to help you to create good quality, and correctly sized, social media images (see Box 11.9 for some examples of popular platforms). These tools often include templates to get you started if you are not graphically inclined.

Although you will want to have some level of consistency across your social media images (e.g., they might all include a link back to your professional website), you should not repeat the same image, over and over, on multiple platforms. Try different templates so that you are creating varied images, especially for those people who may follow you on several different social media sites. Keep in mind that sites like Twitter and Facebook will accept images that you create, but they can also grab images from websites that you post links to. If you plan to link to a blog post, a

BOX 11.9.
Social media image creation platforms.

- Adobe Spark: https://spark.adobe.com
- Canva: https://canva.com
- Desygner: https://desygner.com
- Diptic: http://mac.dipticapp.com
- Easil: http://about.easil.com
- Infogram: https://infogr.am
- Pablo by Buffer: https://pablo.buffer.com
- Recite: http://recite.com
- RELAY: https://relaythat.com
- Ripl: http://ripl.com
- Typorama: www.apperto.com/typorama
- Venngage: https://venngage.com

BOX 11.10.

Social media image augmentation apps.

- Color Splash: www.pcketpixels.com/ColorSplash.html
- Prisma: http://prisma-ai.com
- Word Swag: www.wordswag.co

BOX 11.11.

Tools for measuring the impact of your online presence.

- Iconosquare: https://wwwpro.iconosquare.com/ (Instagram)
- Kred: http://home.kred
- LikeAlyzer: http://likealyzer.com (Facebook)

video, or other information about something you have produced, you will want to make sure the site has a good featured image associated with it to draw people in. See Box 11.10 for some popular image augmentation apps that can help you edit images for social media posting.

Measuring Success

There are several ways to measure the popularity of your posts across platforms. Most social media platforms offer their own custom analytics that you can track, but the most common is the number of followers whom you have and the increase in that number over time. For more specific examples of tools that can help you measure the success of your online presence, including some that are platform specific and some that are fee based, see Box 11.11.

As you can see, there is a wide range of possibilities when it comes to promoting your work online. You can also visit the book's companion website to find additional examples of academics and higher education professionals using the platforms described in this chapter. If you decide to dive in to any of these platforms yourself, I want to hear about it! E-mail contact@katielinder.work to share what you are producing.

CONCLUSION

Three Examples From Higher Education Professionals

With Kevin Gannon, Lee Skallerup Bessette, and Anonymous

A Spectrum of Online Engagement

This conclusion was so fun to put together because it gave me an excuse to ask a few of my favorite colleagues to share in depth about their experiences with being online as academics. Like the profiles woven throughout the book, these essays are meant to offer real-life examples of how academics and higher education professionals are choosing to be online. In this conclusion, you will hear from people who have received amazing opportunities through their online relationships as well as from someone who has chosen to opt out of the digital world—as much as that is possible—altogether. There is a wide spectrum of online engagement happening in academia and these essays will give you a sense of what some of those engagements look like and how they have developed over time.

As you read through these narratives, I hope that you will also consider your own choices regarding online engagement, how your digital identity has changed over time, and what you think your online presence will look like in the future. Although these essays offer just a few glimpses into the stories of academic and higher education professionals online, all of us have our own stories to share, our own rationales for being online, and our own goals for what we are hoping to accomplish. To be sure, these narratives are neither broadly representative nor all-encompassing, but they do offer some interesting insights about how and why being a higher education professional online matters in today's digital age.

Online Presence as Dialectic Process

Kevin Gannon

Kevin Gannon is director of the Center for Excellence in Teaching and Learning (CETL) and professor of history at Grand View University in Des Moines, Iowa. You can find him most easily online at www.thetattooedprof.com (professional website) and https://twitter.com/TheTattooedProf (Twitter).

When anyone in academia tells me social media is a waste of time, I tell the story about how I came to appear in an Oscar-nominated documentary because of Twitter. I'm pretty active on Twitter (@TheTattooedProf), and one afternoon in September 2015, I unleashed a barrage of threaded tweets registering my strong disagreement with an op-ed from that day's *New York Times* written by a prominent historian about the relationship between the U.S. Constitution and slavery (Wilentz, 2015). That "tweetstorm" was retweeted by a number of historians (the #twitterstorians hashtag is a lively community of academics on Twitter), and I was asked by one of them if I wanted to expand on my original thoughts in the form of a guest post on the early American history blog for which he was a coeditor. Sure, I replied, and submitted my post later that day (Gannon, 2015). There was a nice back-and-forth in the blog's comment section, and I figured that would be it—it's not like scholarly debates on a history blog move the needle very much in the larger social media landscape, right? But the next evening, I received a direct message on Twitter from a producer working with Ava DuVernay. They were starting on a new project and had seen my essay as well as checked out some of the other work I'd published on my own blog. As a historian writing on issues addressed in this documentary project, she asked, would I be interested in interviewing on camera as part of this project? Well . . . sure, I replied, sort of amazed that my rage-tweet-become-blog-post had apparently traveled this far. That was the beginning of my association with *13th*, the Netflix original documentary that so powerfully conveys the tangled historical legacies and current realities of race and mass incarceration in the United States. I was privileged enough to attend the film's premier at the New York Film Festival and, as a result of my appearance in the documentary, have had the opportunity to speak to and work with various audiences on campuses across the country. And that's how a series of 20 or so tweets about the Constitution and slavery changed the arc of my academic career.

I'm not exaggerating when I say that every professional opportunity I've had in the last few years—and those have been exponentially more frequent than before—has come from my having an active digital presence. I'd been on Facebook for years, with the love/hate relationship that platform seems to frequently inspire. But in 2013, I joined Twitter, and the following spring, I started my own blog (www.thetattoo edprof.com). At first, Twitter was a place for me to goof around—silly animal GIFs, connecting with fellow baseball and death metal fans, that kind of stuff. I started the blog as a way to coax myself into a more regular writing practice, to create a space for myself to throw out half-baked ideas and work through questions and problems with which I was engaged in more formal projects. But I quickly became aware of, and connected with, an active community of scholars and teachers on Twitter and realized just how vibrant the online scholarly community really is. I connected my blog to my Twitter account, so new posts would automatically be tweeted out, and soon saw that more and more people were reading my posts. Soon, an occasional comment even appeared! My musings on history, teaching, and technology began to intersect with larger conversations in these fields, and my thinking and writing were both helped immeasurably as a result.

Moreover, documentary films aren't the only opportunities that have arisen from my blogging. I've been invited to contribute chapters or essays to books on topics ranging from nineteenth-century U.S. history to academic career advice to flipped learning pedagogy. I have chaired sessions at national conferences that began as Twitter conversations. I've had posts picked up by national news sites, like Vox. com. Two book projects in which I'm currently engaged began as blog posts; for one of those projects, I was contacted by the press's editor to write for a series based on a post that spread through other blogs and was the subject of a higher-ed podcast. Most of the workshops and lectures I've been invited to give the last couple of years started from a conversation that usually went something like "I saw the post you wrote on. . . . And was wondering if you'd be interested in being our guest for . . ."

All of this, and I'm not even doing the stuff that "content marketing professionals" would tell you to do. I don't have search engine optimization for my blog. I share my posts through social media (primarily Twitter), but I don't have any sort of "brand" or "strategy." Indeed, I've been asked what my "Twitter strategy" is, and I don't really know how to answer that question beyond "I yell stuff on the Internet. . . . Oh, and cat GIFs." My scholarly work spans several distinct areas: pedagogy, technology, history, and social justice. It's eclectic, and an eclectic collection of media seems to be the best way for me to engage in those conversations, as well as highlight my own participation to an interested audience—an audience that itself spans a number of fields. As my online profile has grown, I've been able to make connections and participate in conversations that I would never have been a part of had I stayed in the lane I came out of grad school in. In this sense, having an online scholarly presence has taken my scholarly work in directions that I could not have anticipated, which in turn has taken my online presence into new realms and communities as well. It's become quite the dialectical process, to be honest, and it's absolutely rejuvenated my scholarship, my teaching, and the quality of my academic career.

Not everything is unicorns and rainbows online, however, and we ought to be aware of potential pitfalls as we create and maintain our online presence. For instance, as a White cisgen male, my encounters with trolls, twitter eggs, and other denizens of the digital underworld are more limited and unfold on far different terms than what I have seen all too often with colleagues and friends who identify as female or people of color. As with any public space, and that surely includes academic spaces, there are sometimes instances where already privileged voices seek to claim more of the spotlight, or where bullying, abuse, or other forms of harassing behavior occur. I've had to, for example, fend off trolls and hostile e-mails (even one to my university's president!) in response to pieces I've written on topics like the Confederate flag or safe spaces and trigger warnings in higher education. And whether this bad behavior happens in face-to-face or online venues, it is incumbent on us to hold ourselves and others accountable to basic standards of decency and collegiality.

But I would also submit that although there are bad behaviors in some online spaces, the democratizing potential of these spaces far outweighs these potential concerns. Blogs, social media, online journals—all of these have fundamentally changed the nature of scholarly platforms. One does not need to hold a tenured post at an elite institution, or have a passel of monographs on one's CV, to have a seat at the table for the conversations that shape scholarly fields and the educational environment in which one's research is conducted and disseminated. Those of us who teach at colleges or universities much more modest in resources and reputation, or who are contingent faculty, independent scholars, or "alt-ac," now possess the same means to claim our seats, too. My experience has been that research can become more networked, that conversations are more collaboration and less posturing, and that cross-pollination between disciplines can flourish in online spaces.

To effectively cultivate those types of experiences, I've tried to be authentic, open, and honest online. I don't have much of a filter, and that's evident in my writing as well as in my other, less formal, interactions. (I remind myself always of the need to be mindful of what I'm saying, and how I'm saying it. Honesty and authenticity cannot be a license for boorishness.) Having an active online presence, where I am seen as both a scholar and a human being, where I can engage with others in those same capacities, has been not just an asset to my career, but something that has sustained and rewarded me in a variety of ways. It's made me a better scholar, teacher, and practitioner in this diverse and complex space we call higher education.

99k Tweets

Lee Skallerup Bessette
Lee Skallerup Bessette is a learning design specialist at Georgetown University. You can find her most easily online at http://readywriting.org/ (professional website) and https://twitter.com/readywriting (Twitter).

It took me 99k tweets to get a job and change careers within academia.

That, of course, is a gross oversimplification of what happened, of how I went from being a contingent faculty member at a rural, regional, state institution to a job in faculty development at an R1, flagship institution. My prolific Twitter activity was fueled by hundreds of blog posts and other writing that I did for a variety of publications and organizations, as well as participation in numerous Twitter "chats," and generally being really good at connecting people with ideas, research, and other resources.

I have always been a writer, someone who could put words together prolifically and somewhat well. I wrote press releases for my swim team in high school. I edited our school newspaper and supervised moving it online. I used to write for a friend's website—what would now be considered a blog, but at the time it was more like a zine—back when I had been an undergraduate. Then those in my PhD program told me that no one would take me seriously because of my presence on the web. So I gave it all up, and just about any and all writing that wasn't directly related to my graduate student work stopped.

Fast-forward almost a decade. There was nothing particularly special about me when I got on Twitter and started a blog in 2010. I was a part of the glut of PhDs in the humanities, specializing in an area that could best be described as niche, impacted by the economics of higher education. I had very two young children and a husband who had just started on the tenure track, and I was underemployed. I started a blog and got on Twitter because I had nothing else to do and no one else to talk to. I was frustrated from feeling silenced and stymied.

I was hungry, I was angry, and I was naïve. I already felt like I had lost everything professionally, so there was nothing left for me to lose. What comes out of those early interactions on Twitter and posts on my blog is someone who is all three of those things, coupled with someone who had a deep love of teaching and the power and potential of higher education. My teaching experience thus far had been at teaching-intensive, public, regional universities that served various nontraditional and at-risk student populations. I was first-generation myself, but largely privileged, having attended a university that typically attracted other first-generation, rural, and working-class students. Although I cared deeply about my scholarship, I cared more about my students' educations and the future of higher education. It was an area that we were largely taught to ignore (or at least until we achieved tenure) as we were professionalized in graduate school.

I threw myself into my work. I always want to make sure that I make this clear when I talk about those early years blogging and tweeting: I considered that to be my full-time, or at least primary, job. My kids napped consistently and regularly and went to bed early. My husband was busy in the first years of a tenure-track job. My life, to a large extent, became my blog and Twitter. It was both a job and a lifeline. It wasn't sustainable in the long run, but at the time, it was what I devoted the intellectual and affective energy I had previously been putting into my scholarship and my teaching.

I found, very quickly, that I was somehow built for Twitter. I could skim the constant firehose stream of my timeline and retain a surprising amount. It also freed me to explore all of my various disparate interests, interests that I had suppressed or ignored in my all-encompassing journey to a PhD and a tenure-track job. Teaching, a topic that is often not discussed, or at least not openly and critically, was a central topic for many of the people I initially followed; teachers were some of the earliest adopters of Twitter as a professional development tool. I found I was also able to keep the various disparate people and feeds that I followed straight and connect them with one another when I found something I knew would be of interest to them. I became someone who was known to engage, connect, and provide useful resources and information. Twitter chats, hashtags, large-scale conversations. . . . I loved and embraced all of it.

My presence on Twitter (and on my blog) then led to a number of opportunities to write for different audiences and platforms. I said yes to almost any and every opportunity to write and be published, paid or not (and usually not). I've since rethought that stance, but at the time, I was more interested in exposure than fair compensation. I was lucky enough that my husband had a decent job that covered most of our bills, and I managed to get some freelance and research work to cover the rest, before moving into a full-time non-tenure-track position at the same institution. Again, the approach I took here isn't sustainable, nor is it one I would ever recommend anyone do. But it did mean, in some very specific instances, that I was able to keep building my network, which directly led to my blog moving to *Inside Higher Ed*, as well as a number of other well-paid writing jobs.

As my network expanded, I found a wider variety of possibilities within academia for career paths. I "discovered" what was then being called *alt-ac positions*—jobs within academia that provided an intellectually rewarding experience and *stability*. These jobs often were adjacent to the digital humanities (DH), which meshed my humanities training with my longtime interest with technology (particularly in the classroom). I learned from my peers all over the country and all over the world, and embraced digital pedagogy as my ethos and my approach to teaching. What I had long wanted to do, who I had long wanted to be as an academic and an educator, were coming together.

But my DH credentials were self-taught, underfunded, and undersupported. I was still alone, at my regional, state, teaching-intensive institution teaching off the tenure track, and they could have cared less about what I was doing, despite connecting with and being a part of a large, international DH project (an opportunity I got through someone I knew from Twitter). I was furiously writing, connecting, searching for a way out. A colleague from my PhD program had relatively recently moved into faculty development, and I started to ask him questions (or maybe he started to prompt me to ask those questions) as to what being in faculty development involved. My public scholarship on teaching and technology, coupled with my PhD, made me an ideal candidate for a position in a teaching and learning center or a teaching with technology shop. This was a new alt-ac possibility I hadn't previously been aware of.

And my network came through for me. When I publicly expressed an interest in moving into faculty development, one of my followers on Twitter reached out to me, giving me both support and the resources necessary to make the transition. When my family decided to move from the rural college town we had been living in to the nearest city, another follower reached out and gave me my first job in faculty development.

I checked my stats on Twitter when that happened. 99k tweets.

There were also a couple of hundred blog posts, thousands and thousands of words written across the web on various platforms and outlets. It took me a long time to settle on faculty development, and in the meantime, I had written about digital humanities, social media, academic branding, blogging, as well as edited two books on authors I had studied.

Twitter literally changed my life, for the better. It was the space for me not only to get that job, to get me where I am now professionally, but also to embrace the various facets of my personality, as well as professional and personal interests. I like to say I am the most myself on Twitter. Twitter and my blog were two powerful tools for me to write and rewrite myself in ways that felt right for me, rather than what academia wanted to make me into. I also had a tremendous amount of privilege, which enabled me to be able to take the risks that I did and continue to do. I try to make sure that I use that privilege to help others find their space and place in academia through social media.

As I write this (March 2017), it has been exactly seven years since I started my blog and created my Twitter self, @readywriting. I look back, and I am still a little bit in disbelief that any of this even happened. I found friends on Twitter, as well—real friends, with whom I have shared the struggles, successes, and everything in between, and them with me. We have watched our careers grow and change, and our families grow and change. We have lived in each other's words and pictures and lives 140 characters at a time. I don't know what concrete advice I would have to "manage" any of this. There was no plan, or rather, the original plan was quickly tossed aside for the ride that this has been.

My "Pinned Tweet" that appears permanently at the top of my profile reads: "I wrote myself into existence, literally, from early journaling to what you see here." If I had any advice to offer, it's to take the opportunity to write yourself into existence, particularly if academia wants to deny your right or your ability to do just that.

On the Question of an Academic Online Identity

Professor Anonymous

Professor Anonymous is a midcareer academic, tenured associate professor, and department chair who works at a liberal arts non-Tier-1 school in a large U.S. city.

I have chosen to withhold my name from this publication to make the point—explicitly—that it is not my aim to gain recognition, nor to add another publication to my CV with this essay. I write it because I feel I have something important to share on the topic and am grateful to Katie Linder for approaching me and giving me this opportunity.

Unlike the other contributors to this conclusion, I have opted not to develop an online identity (academic or otherwise). In this day and age this is often looked down on, as your employer most likely would like to have a picture of you on the website and use you for marketing purposes in other ways, if appropriate. I am walking the fine line of trying to remain in control of myself by limiting the (re)sources I permit others to have over me. The two issues implied are the relationship between control of oneself and commodification choices of one's work. I want to spend the following pages outlining cultural and situational reasons for why an online identity may or may not be attractive to a faculty member.

Academic branding is a form of marketing—whether via social media or in an old-fashioned way, such as in-person networking at a conference. My aim is to be known for quality work in my areas of expertise, for both niche and general audiences, pending publication. Although one creates an online persona for most likely a very similar reason, aiming to build expert status in one's area of research and/or expertise over time, the online environment, and particular social media platforms, add an additional dimension and level of potential interaction as the previous two essays have shown. There are several questions faculty and higher education professionals need to ask themselves: Should one have one's own website? What social media accounts should one have? How often should one update one's Twitter feed? Should one retweet work of colleagues? Should pictures be posted? If yes, professional, personal? Staged or not? And so on.

Ultimately, the aim is to have positive recognition in one's field with such benefits as being approached for speeches or other kinds of presentations, publications, and the like, and to establish connections with colleagues. Without a doubt, the interactions with "stranger colleagues" across the web are more frequent than they were prior to the Internet, but has positive value been added to one's career?

As a researcher, my interest lies with the author's research and contributions to my areas of study. The author's name has the signification to link with other academic work. I am reminded of Michel Foucault's (1969) work "What Is an Author?" According to Foucault, an author has four functions: creating designation, designation permitting categorization for grouping purposes, categorization producing the potential of cultural status, and text being provided with signification by being linked to a specific author (as summarized by Staiger, 2003, p. 28). These functions have been implied in my discussion in the previous paragraphs. Thus, even with the evolution of technology, the functions of authorship arguably have stayed the same; they still hold true in the social media age/digital age/online identity age.

Further, Staiger (2003) summarizes Foucault's argument that author signification can lead to "punishing" or "rewarding individuals on the basis of what they write" (p. 28). This behavior fits with a culture that places a high emphasis on individualism, Staiger argues. I view Staiger's extension of Foucault's argument as one of the driving forces behind many academics who build academic online identities. The United States has a very high individualism score. According to Geert Hofstede (2017b), the U.S. individualism index is 91, meaning that people are expected to be self-reliant and that although an emphasis on equal rights exists, a hierarchy is established, which makes marketing oneself (potentially) necessary to climb a career ladder (p. 7). One is responsible for oneself and for one's own success or failure. The saying "keeping up with the Joneses" comes to mind; it no longer only applies to one's personal domain but also to one's professional career.

The country I grew up in has a significantly lower individualism score (though it has been rising over the past decade as the culture has evolved, according to Hofstede). Approximately a decade ago, the country I grew up in was listed as being a collectivist country, with a tendency toward individualism. As of March 2017, it is being classified as individualistic. (Having visited regularly and following the news almost daily, I have observed the cultural change.) The different ideology I grew up in may be a factor for why I have such a different viewpoint on the new possibilities of a professional online presence. As summarized by Hofstede (2017a), collectivistic cultures focus on "the group," on "long-term commitment," and on "loyalty" (p. 5).

I find myself collaborating on articles with colleagues; with many I have coauthored more than once. And even if we don't coauthor, I am part of a group of colleagues who support one another in research, writing, and teaching. We have made a long-term commitment to one another and meet in person regularly (usually once per month). At these meetings, we discuss our respective research progress and other relevant faculty matters. However, many of my colleagues, even when meeting is a possibility, prefer asynchronous e-mail conversations. Why don't people (want to) meet anymore?

I picked up Sherry Turkle's (2016) *Reclaiming Conversation* at the suggestion of a colleague. Among many great examples, she describes a scenario where team members don't show up for in-person meetings, yet one complains about having an issue with a client. The manager suggests an in-person meeting with the client; this recommendation surprises the team member. In this example, the conclusion drawn is focused on age. "Younger colleagues have grown up thinking that electronic communication is a universal language" (p. 262). Yet brainstorming, for instance, can work much more effectively in person than in asynchronous e-mail conversations. The monthly meetings with my colleagues are precisely so fruitful because we consciously dedicate our agreed-upon meeting times to one another, permitting us to listen, ponder, and converse without disruption.

However, working in harmony with others may also mean that one has to share the credit, which may not be seen as desirable by some. For example, I worked with two colleagues organizing a series of events. One of my colleagues—older and having been employed at the university for longer than I have—had the opportunity to be interviewed by a major newspaper, and he wanted my "okay" that he could label himself as the sole founder and organizer of the series. I did not give him the okay. I said that we all cofounded and co-organized the series and shared the work. He was not pleased, but as I read in the finished article, he had labeled himself as a cofounder and co-organizer.

Arguably, individualism also impacts the phenomenon that social media has created regarding the power of making or breaking somebody's career. If one has been captured doing something controversial, chances are people will "put it out there" and discuss the person in negative ways. It gives someone a possibility to supersede that person, to possibly take his or her place. This returns me to the reasons people seek a professional identity. It appears to be another way of "keeping up with the Joneses," to gain that step ahead, to achieve recognition that will (hopefully) assist with economic gain in the long run. Competition is part of an individualistic mindset, and social media has provided another field in which to compete. I choose to #optout.

For me, ironically, not having an online presence and not advertising my research in any other way—for instance, by having it highlighted on my employer's web page—has led to this publication. But how did I make the connection? How did Katie hear of me?

Without giving away specifics, I network in person and via e-mail. I am fortunate to be teaching in a major U.S. city with many places of higher education, permitting me to be in touch easily with colleagues across the entire spectrum, from Tier-1 research institutions to community colleges. I certainly would have to reconsider my position on using the Internet as a way of networking were I to move to a place of employment in a rural area. Also, I have to admit, even when having campuses within an hour of one another, once a connection has been established, Skype has become a great tool for face-to-face conversation.

Budget constraints at my place of employment limit me to an average of one conference per year, which restricts the opportunity to network at such events. The decreased possibilities of funding from my own institution have definitely impacted my ability to meet others, in my discipline as well as outside my area. (I have published numerous interdisciplinary articles with colleagues from other subject areas; subject-specific conferences are of limited value for those.) However, in-person networking over the past decade as well as relationships with editors at publications have created established connections. Apparently, people do think of me and my work, and I am recommended via word of mouth.

These recommendations also tend to be rather fruitful. People who do contact me have some in-depth knowledge about my work, and thus the chances of collaboration are very high as we are likely a good match. Yes, I get contacted much less than my colleagues on social media, but the quality of my contacts is high. Quality over quantity is one of my mantras.

This links with another mantra of mine—the creation of a healthy work-life balance. I have clearly defined working hours. I work to live—that is to say, I am not married to my work. I like what I do for work very much, but I love what I do in my spare time. I gain much more fulfillment from the latter than the former. Outside of working hours, I minimize Internet distraction. Labeling the Internet as a distraction already suggests the attitude I have toward this mode of connecting and communicating. I have observed how many of my friends have permitted social media to control their lives. They need to inform their online friends of their whereabouts; need to know whether a comment has been "liked"; and, in relation to academia, check whether they have received positive responses about a tweet from colleagues they have never met. I have also noticed that they are impacted on an emotional level if communication is received that was not to their liking. I opt out of this potential source of stress.

Although I have provided my viewpoint on the social media landscape in relation to an academic identity, I do believe that certain forms of interaction are beneficial at different times in one's academic career. As a department chair, I have more service obligations and less time for scholarship. I made that choice consciously, as I do like the management side of higher education. Thus, I am very selective about the research work I focus on and produce less than some of my colleagues.

Also, were I a junior faculty member, especially living abroad or in a rural area in the United States, I wouldn't be surprised if I chose to create a limited online identity—that is, to select one or two mechanisms to market myself. After all, during a job search, every department looks at the work available online by all job candidates. Thus, I do understand and support colleagues who are engrained in commodifying themselves online. I view not having an online identity as a privilege.

Some Closing Thoughts

One of the themes of this book that is illustrated particularly well through this conclusion is the range of reasons why academics choose to be—or not to be—online. Online presence is a highly personal choice that is often impacted by identity, career stage, employment status, discipline, family responsibilities and obligations, personal and professional values, need for community, and many other factors. The earlier chapters in this book may have helped you to explore these areas for yourself, but these essays—as well as the profiles included throughout the book—offer a glimpse into the decision-making processes of academics and higher education professionals who are situated in a diverse range of disciplinary, institutional, identity, and life contexts.

I hope that reading these stories encourages you to ask your colleagues about how and why they are online in the ways that they have chosen, and also to consider sharing your own story about the decisions you have made about your professional online presence. Join the conversation about academic digital identity using #acdigid on your social media platform of choice to share your story.

GLOSSARY

1Password (https://1password.com/) a password management tool

Academia.edu (https://www.academia.edu/) a social media platform where academics and higher education professionals can share research and other scholarly artifacts and follow the research of others

Adobe Connect (http://www.adobe.com/products/adobeconnect.html) a webinar platform

Adobe Spark (https://spark.adobe.com/) a social media image creation tool

AllTop (http://alltop.com/) a news aggregation site

Altmetric (https://altmetric.com/) a tool for measuring scholarly impact via social media

Amazon Author Page (https://authorcentral.amazon.com/) an option for authors who have books sold through the Amazon platform to create a profile that shares information about the author and a list of other published works

App mini software applications on mobile devices that are designed to complete a specific task or function

Blog a "web log" where authors can post ideas or content on a particular topic

Blogger (https://www.blogger.com/) a blogging platform

Bluehost (https://www.bluehost.com/) a registrar where you can search for and purchase domain names

Brand a combination of textual and visual items, signs, and symbols that create an association with a product or person that differentiates that product or person from others like them

BrandYourself (https://brandyourself.com/) a software tool to help improve the Google search results connected to your name and online identity

Browser an application used for viewing web pages

Buffer (https://buffer.com/) a social media scheduling platform

Camera+ (http://camera.plus/) a photo app for mobile devices that improves image quality

Canva (https://www.canva.com/) a social media image creation tool

ClickToTweet (https://clicktotweet.com/) a free online service that allows you to create a link that will automatically add predrafted content to a Twitter status box when someone clicks on the link you have created

Color Splash (http://www.pocketpixels.com/ColorSplash.html) a colorization app for mobile devices that allows you to augment a photo to be black and white with specific detail areas in color

Constant Contact (https://www.constantcontact.com/) an e-mail marketing platform where users can build e-mail lists, create e-mails with predrafted templates, and automate messages to people on their e-mail lists

Content management system (CMS) a tool used to manage data for building web pages

ConvertKit (https://convertkit.com/) an e-mail marketing platform where users can build e-mail lists, create e-mails with predrafted templates, and automate messages to people on their e-mail lists

Creative Commons (https://creativecommons.org/) a form of copyright licensing that includes six different options for sharing work; each license is denoted by a symbol that can be added to a print work, web resource, or other creation

Crowdcast (https://www.crowdcast.io/) a webinar platform

Desygner (https://desygner.com/) a social media image creation tool

Digg Reader (http://digg.com/reader) an RSS feed aggregator

Diptic (http://mac.dipticapp.com/) a social media image creation tool that allows you to create photo collages

Disqus (https://disqus.com/) a website plug-in for managing comments

Domain name the address for a website

DreamHost (https://www.dreamhost.com/) a registrar provider and web hosting company

Drupal (https://www.drupal.org/) an open-source content management system

Easil (http://about.easil.com/) a social media image creation tool

Edgar (https://app.meetedgar.com/) a social media scheduling platform

E-mail a digital system to share messages

Everystockphoto (http://www.everystockphoto.com) a collection of searchable free digital images

Facebook (https://www.facebook.com/) a social media platform where you can create a profile, page, or group and connect with others to share updates, photos, and prerecorded and live video

Facebook Live a video tool that allows users to record video, broadcast live, and then post the video for other Facebook users to replay at a later time

Feedly (https://feedly.com/) an RSS feed aggregator

Flickr (https://www.flickr.com/) an online photograph management and sharing application

Flickr Creative Commons (https://www.flickr.com/creativecommons/) a way to search for photographs in the Flickr collection based on type of copyright license

Fotolia (https://us.fotolia.com/) a collection of searchable digital images

Friends+Me (https://friendsplus.me/) a social media scheduling platform for Google+

Futurity (http://www.futurity.org/) a news aggregation site that collects research news from universities

GetResponse (https://www.getresponse.com/) an e-mail marketing platform where users can build e-mail lists, create e-mails with predrafted templates, and automate messages to people on their e-mail lists

GIF (graphic interchange format) a series of images overlaid upon one another to create the illusion of a short animation or moving image

GoDaddy (https://www.godaddy.com/) a registrar provider and web hosting company

Goodreads (https://www.goodreads.com/) a social media platform where you can log and share with other users the books you are currently reading, have previously read, or want to read in the future; review books and read others' book reviews; or create an author page if you have published a book

Google+ (https://plus.google.com/) a social media platform where users can post text-based updates, images, and videos and connect with and follow other users

Google Hangouts (https://hangouts.google.com/) a video chat tool that allows users to record video conversations, broadcast the video live, and then post the video for other viewers to replay at a later time

Google Scholar (https://scholar.google.com/) a public profile that aggregates a user's published scholarship and logs citation rates

GoToWebinar (https://www.gotomeeting.com/webinar) a webinar platform

Hashtag a symbol (#) used to mark a word or phrase so that it creates a link to other content using that marked word or phrase

Holy Kaw (http://holykaw.alltop.com/) a news aggregation site

Hootsuite (https://hootsuite.com/) a social media scheduling platform

HostGator (http://www.hostgator.com/) a registrar where you can search for and purchase domain names

Iconosquare (https://pro.iconosquare.com/) an analytics tool for Instagram users

IFTTT (https://ifttt.com/) a free online tool that allows users to create "recipes" to automate services between a range of other online tools

Impactstory (https://impactstory.org/) an open-source website that helps researchers to track and share the online impacts of their research on social media channels

Infogram (https://infogr.am/) an online tool to create infographics, charts, and maps using premade templates and designs

Instagram (https://www.instagram.com/) a social media platform that primarily focuses on the sharing of images and short live and prerecorded videos

Instagram Stories an Instagram feature that allows users to record and share short videos that are posted for only 24 hours

Instatag (http://instatag.net/) a collection of the most popular Instagram hashtags

iStockPhoto (http://www.istockphoto.com/) a collection of searchable digital images

Kred (http://home.kred/) an online service for measuring a person's online impact

LastPass (https://www.lastpass.com/) a password management tool

LikeAlyzer (http://likealyzer.com/) an online service for measuring the impact of Facebook pages

LinkedIn (https://www.linkedin.com/) a social media platform for professionals from a range of fields who create the equivalent of a CV or résumé as their online profile; users can recommend one another, seek out employers or employees, and endorse one another for skills and abilities

Logo a visual mark or symbol to promote brand recognition

MailChimp (https://mailchimp.com/) an e-mail marketing platform where users can build e-mail lists, create e-mails with predrafted templates, and automate messages to people on their e-mail lists

Mastermind groups small communities of people who meet to share resources based on their career stage or interest in a particular topic

Medium (https://medium.com/) a group blogging platform where users can post their long-form essays, tag them, attract followers, and follow and comment on others' work

Meme a humorous digital artifact (text, image, video, or otherwise) that is created and spread across the Internet, often with slight variations

Moldiv (http://www.jellybus.com/moldiv) a photo app for mobile devices that improves image quality

Namecheap (https://www.namecheap.com/) a registrar where you can search for and purchase domain names

Network Solutions (https://www.networksolutions.com/) a registrar provider and web hosting company

Noun Project (https://thenounproject.com/) an online collection of icons that can be freely used or purchased

Open Science Data Cloud (OSDC) (https://www.opensciencedatacloud.org/) an online platform for researchers across disciplines to store and share data

ORCID (http://orcid.org/) an online platform for researchers that provides a persistent digital identity that distinguishes one's research and data from that of others

Pablo (https://pablo.buffer.com/) a social media image creation platform available via Buffer where users can create social media images using predrafted templates that match the size requirements of a range of social media platforms

Periscope (https://www.periscope.tv/) a platform to stream and record live video

Pinterest (https://www.pinterest.com/) a social media platform where users can "pin" images to "boards" to create collections, share those collections with other users, and "repin" images from other users' boards

Podcast primarily audio recordings that can also include video; podcasts are easily transferable to mobile devices

Populagram (https://websta.me/tag/populagram) an analytics platform for Instagram

Post Planner (http://www.postplanner.com/) a fee-based social marketing platform

Prisma (http://prisma-ai.com/) a photo app that allows you to use filters to change your photos to the styles of various artists

Proboards (https://www.proboards.com/) a free discussion board hosting platform

Recite (http://recite.com/) a social media image creation platform that focuses on the creation of quote-based images

Reclaim Hosting (https://reclaimhosting.com/) a web hosting service for academics and institutions of higher education

Reddit (https://www.reddit.com/) a news aggregation site

RelayThat (https://relaythat.com/) a social media image creation platform

ResearchGate (https://www.researchgate.net/home) a social platform where researchers can share their publications with other researchers and pose questions related to research that can be answered by other users

Ripl (http://ripl.com/) an app to create social media images

RSS real simple syndication pushes content out from web sources such as blogs or podcasts through a feed that can get read by RSS programs

Slack (https://slack.com/) a web- and app-based messaging system

SlidesCarnival (http://www.slidescarnival.com/) a collection of free presentation slide templates for Google slide users

SlideShare (http://www.slideshare.net/) a platform where users can upload and share PowerPoint presentations and other documents in a public or private forum

SmartBrief (http://www.smartbrief.com/) a news aggregation website

Snapchat (https://www.snapchat.com/) an app for mobile devices that allows users to record and share video content that is available for only a short period of time

Social media web-hosted spaces where people connect to share information and collaborate on ideas; common social media platforms are Twitter and Facebook

SoundCloud (http://www.soundcloud.com) a social media site for sharing and listening to audio files

Sprout Social (http://sproutsocial.com/) a social media management tool

Squarespace (https://www.squarespace.com/) a website creation platform with registrar and web hosting services

Stocksy (https://www.stocksy.com/) a collection of royalty-free searchable digital images

StumbleUpon (http://www.stumbleupon.com/) an aggregation' site for interesting web content

TagsForLikes (http://tagsforlikes.com/) an app that shares the most popular Instagram hashtags and allows you to easily copy and paste multiple hashtags into photo descriptions

Tailwind (https://www.tailwindapp.com/) a social media scheduling platform for Pinterest and Instagram

TChat (http://www.tchat.io/) a tool for more efficient and easier Twitter chats

TED (https://www.ted.com/) a website housing a collection of inspirational videos from expert speakers in a range of disciplines

The Old Reader (https://theoldreader.com/) an RSS feed aggregator

Triberr (http://triberr.com/) a community for bloggers to share content and to find other bloggers with similar content

Troll a person who intentionally tries to provoke others in online settings by posting negative, off-topic, or argumentative messages

Tumblr (https://www.tumblr.com/) a blogging platform

TweetDeck (https://tweetdeck.twitter.com/) a social media management platform for Twitter that allows you to simultaneously see separate accounts, hashtags, and notifications

Twitter (https://twitter.com/) a social media "microblogging" platform where users can post "tweet" updates of 140 characters or less; tweets can also include GIFs and other images

Twitter chat a form of conversation via the social media platform Twitter where users have a real-time discussion using the same hashtag

Twubs (http://twubs.com/) a platform for following hashtags and hosting tweet chats

Typeform (https://www.typeform.com/) an online service to create web forms that can also be embedded into other websites

Typorama (http://www.apperto.com/typorama/) an app for creating social media graphics

URL shorteners tools that help to shorten links; examples include bit.ly, goo.gl, tinyurl.com, Buffer, and Hootsuite

Venngage (https://venngage.com/) a platform for creating infographics

Vitae (https://chroniclevitae.com/) a platform created by *The Chronicle of Higher Education* as an "online career hub" for academics and higher education professionals

Wavve (http://www.getwavve.com/) a platform for creating sharable social media content for audio

Web browser an application used for viewing web pages

Web hosting the process through which you rent web space

WebX (https://www.webex.com/) a webinar platform

Wikimedia Commons (https://commons.wikimedia.org/) an online repository of free-use images and other media

Wikiquote (https://en.wikiquote.org/) an online repository of quotations

WiseStamp (http://www.wisestamp.com/) a platform for designing professional-looking and promotional e-mail signatures

Wix (http://www.wix.com/) a website creation platform with registrar and web hosting services

WordPress (https://wordpress.com/create/) an open-source content management system that also acts as a website creation platform with registrar and web hosting services

Word Swag (http://wordswag.co/) an app for adding text to your photos when creating social media posts

Wufoo (http://www.wufoo.com/) an online service to create web forms that can also be embedded into other websites

YouTube (https://www.youtube.com/) an online hub for posting videos where users can create a "channel" and have subscribers or subscribe and follow other users of the platform

Zoom (https://zoom.us/) a webinar platform

REFERENCES

600 million and counting. (2016). *Instagram.* Retrieved from http://blog.instagram.com/post/154506585127/161215-600million

About Us. (2016). *LinkedIn.* Retrieved from https://press.linkedin.com/about-linkedin

Al-Aufi, A. S., & Fulton, C. (2014). Use of social networking tools for informal scholarly communication in humanities and social sciences disciplines. *Procedia—Social and Behavioral Sciences, 147*, 436–445.

Barbour, K., & Marshall, D. (2012). The academic online: Constructing persona through the World Wide Web. *First Monday, 17*(9). Retrieved from http://journals.uic.edu/ojs/index.php/fm/article/view/3969/3292

Bosch, T. E. (2009). Using online social networking for teaching and learning: Facebook use at the University of Capetown. *Communication, Cultural and Media Studies, 35*(2), 185–200.

Brown, A., Cowan, J., & Green, T. (2016). Faculty productivity: Using social media and measuring its impact. *EDUCAUSE Review.* Retrieved from http://er.educause.edu/articles/2016/5/faculty-productivity-using-social-media-and-measuring-its-impact

Carrigan, M. (2016). *Social media for academics.* Los Angeles, CA: SAGE.

Christakis, N. A., & Fowler, J. H. (2009). *Connected: The surprising power of our social networks and how they shape our lives.* New York, NY: Little, Brown.

Corbyn, Z. (2010). All about me, dot com. *Times Higher Education.* Retrieved from https://www.timeshighereducation.com/features/all-about-me-dot-com/413005.article

Costa, C. (2014). Outcasts on the inside: Academics reinventing themselves online. *International Journal of Lifelong Education, 34*(2), 194–210.

Daniels, J. (2013). From tweet to blog post to peer-reviewed article: How to be a scholar now. *The Impact Blog.* Retrieved from http://blogs.lse.ac.uk/impactofsocialsciences/2013/09/25/how-to-be-a-scholar-daniels/

Davies, J., & Merchant, G. (2006). Looking from the inside out: Academic blogging as new literacy. In M. Knobel & C. Lankshear (Eds.), *A new literacies sampler* (pp. 167–197). New York, NY: Peter Lang.

DiPiazza, F. D. (2012). *Friend me! 600 years of social networking in America.* Minneapolis, MN: Twenty-First Century Books.

Dudenhoffer, C. (2012). Pin it! Pinterest as a library marketing and information literacy tool. *College & Research Libraries News, 73*(6), 328–332.

Duffy, E. D., & Pooley, J. D. (2017, January–March). "Facebook for academics": The convergence of self-branding and social media logic on Academia.edu. *Social Media + Society,* 1–11.

Dunleavy, P. (2015a). Should your academic CV (or résumé) go digital at last? *Medium.* Retrieved from https://medium.com/advice-and-help-in-authoring-a-phd-or-non-fiction/should-your-resum%C3%A9-or-cv-go-digital-at-last-23ef784c013b#.naqldnveb

Dunleavy, P. (2015b). Why academic CVs (or résumés) are distinctive. *Medium.* Retrieved from https://medium.com/advice-and-help-in-authoring-a-phd-or-non-fiction/why-academic-cvs-and-resum%C3%A9s-are-distinctive-ba36162c0d04#.zbsnqy5d5

Egan, G. (2016). Why academics should NOT take time for social media. *Times Higher Education*. Retrieved from https://www.timeshighereducation.com/blog/why-academics-should-not-make-time-social-media

Estes, H. (2012). Blogging and academic identity. *Literature Compass, 9*(12), 974–982.

Eysenbach, G. (2011). Can tweets predict citations? Metrics of social impact based on Twitter and correlation with traditional metrics of scientific impact. *Journal of Medical Internet Research, 13*(4), e123.

Farmer, B., Yue, A., & Brooks, C. (2008). Using blogging for higher order learning in large cohort university teaching: A case study. *Australasian Journal of Educational Technology, 24*(2), 123–136.

Ferber, A. (2017). Faculty under attack. *Humboldt Journal of Social Relations, 1*(39), 37–42.

Fertik, M., & Thompson, D. C. (2015). *The reputation economy: How to optimize your digital footprint in a world where your reputation is your most valuable asset.* New York, NY: Crown.

Flaherty, C. (2017a). Belly of the beast. *Inside Higher Ed.* Retrieved from https://www.insidehighered.com/news/2017/08/14/sociologists-seek-systematic-response-online-targeting-and-threats-against-public#.WZLsxw0kX7k.facebook

Flaherty, C. (2017b). Old criticisms, new threats. *Inside Higher Ed.* Retrieved from https://www.insidehighered.com/news/2017/06/26/professors-are-often-political-lightning-rods-now-are-facing-new-threats-over-their

Flaherty, C. (2017c). Suspended for standing up to Fox News? *Inside Higher Ed.* Retrieved from https://www.insidehighered.com/news/2017/06/21/college-allegedly-suspends-communications-adjunct-comments-about-race-fox-news

Foucault, M. (1969). What is an author? In James B. Faubion (Ed.), *Aesthetics, method, and epistemology.* Retrieved from http://www.english.upenn.edu/~cavitch/pdf-library/Foucault_Author.pdf

Gannon, K. (2015). Guest post: The constitution, slavery, and the problem of agency [Web log post]. *The Junto: A Group Blog on Early American History.* Retrieved from https://earlyamericanists.com/2015/09/17/constitution-slavery-and-the-problem-of-agency/

Gasman, M. (2016). *Academics going public: How to write and speak beyond academe.* New York, NY: Routledge.

Graham, M. (2013). Social media and the academy: New publics or public geographies? *Dialogues in Human Geography, 3*(1), 77–80.

Grandy, T. (2015). Build a professional website this summer (without HTML). *The Chronicle of Higher Education.* Retrieved from https://www.insidehighered.com/blogs/gradhacker/build-professional-website-summer-without-html

Greenwood, S., Perrin, A., & Duggan, M. (2016). Social media update 2016. *Pew Research Center.* Retrieved from http://www.pewinternet.org/2016/11/11/social-media-update-2016/

Gruzd, A., Staves, K., & Wilk, A. (2011). Tenure and promotion in the age of online social media. *Proceedings of the Association for Information Science and Technology, 48*(1), 1–9.

Guidry, K. R., & Pasquini, L. (2016). Twitter chat as an informal learning tool: A case study using #sachat. In H. Yang & S. Wang (Eds.), *Professional development and workplace learning: Concepts, methodologies, tools, and applications* (pp. 1122–1139). Hershey, PA: Information Science Reference. (Reprint from 2013)

Harzing, A. (2017). Google Scholar is a serious alternative to Web of Science. *The London School of Economics and Political Science Impact Blog.* Retrieved from http://blogs

.lse.ac.uk/impactofsocialsciences/2017/03/16/google-scholar-is-a-serious-alternative-to-web-of-science/

Hitchcock, J. A. (2017). *Cyberbullying and the wild, wild web: What everyone needs to know.* New York, NY: Rowman & Littlefield.

Hoffman, R., & Casnocha, B. (2012). *The start-up of you.* New York, NY: Crown Business.

Hofstede, G. (2017a, March). *National culture.* Retrieved from https://www.hofstede-insights.com/product/compare-countries/

Hofstede, G. (2017b, March). *United States.* Retrieved from https://www.hofstede-insights.com/product/compare-countries/

Hogshead, S. (2014). *How the world sees you.* New York, NY: Harper Business.

Hurt, C., & Yin, T. (2006). Blogging while untenured and other extreme sports. *Washington University Law Review, 84,* 1235–1255.

Jenkins, R. (2016). How to build a following on Twitter—and why you should. *The Chronicle of Higher Education.* Retrieved from http://www.chronicle.com/article/How-to-Build-a-Twitter/235309

Joosten, T. (2012). *Social media for educators: Strategies and best practices.* San Francisco, CA: Jossey-Bass.

Kelsky, K. (2016). How to tailor your online image. *Chronicle Vitae.* Retrieved from https://chroniclevitae.com/news/1027-how-to-tailor-your-online-image

Kirkup, G. (2010, February). Academic blogging: Academic practice and academic identity. *London Review of Education, 8*(1), 75–84.

Kjellberg, S. (2010). I am a blogging researcher: Motivations for blogging in a scholarly context. *First Monday, 15*(8). Retrieved from http://firstmonday.org/ojs/index.php/fm/article/view/2962/2580

Lindemann, M. (2010). The madwoman with a laptop: Notes toward a literary prehistory of academic fem blogging. *Journal of Women's History, 22*(4), 209–219.

Lupton, D., Mewburn, I., & Thompson, P. (2017). *The digital academic: Critical perspectives on digital technologies in higher education.* New York, NY: Routledge.

Mahrt, M., & Puschmann, C. (2014). Science blogging: An exploratory study of motives, styles, and audience reactions. *Journal of Science Communication, 13*(3), 1–17.

Maitzen, R. (2012). Scholarship 2.0: Blogging and/as academic practice. *Journal of Victorian Culture, 17*(3), 348–354.

Malesky, L. A., & Peters, C. (2012). Defining appropriate professional behavior for faculty and university students on social networking websites. *Higher Education, 63*(1), 135–151.

Marwick, A., Blackwell, L., & Lo, K. (2016). Best practices for conducting risky research and protecting yourself from online harassment. *Data & Society.* Retrieved from http://datasociety.net/output/best-practices-for-conducting-risky-research/

Mewburn, I. (2017). Interview: Jessie Daniels. In D. Lupton, I. Mewburn, & P. Thomson (Eds.), *The digital academic: Critical perspectives on digital technologies in higher education.* New York, NY: Routledge.

Mewburn, I., & Thompson, P. (2013). Why do academics blog? An analysis of audiences, purposes and challenges. *Studies in Higher Education, 38*(8), 1105–1119.

Meyers, K. (2013). Manage your digital identity. *ProfHacker Blog.* Retrieved from https://www.insidehighered.com/blogs/gradhacker/manage-your-digital-identity

Miah, A. (2016). Why academics should make time for social media. *Times Higher Education.* Retrieved from https://www.timeshighereducation.com/comment/why-academics-should-make-time-for-social-media-app

Moran, M., Seaman, J., & Tinti-Kane, H. (2012). *Teaching, learning, and sharing: How today's higher education faculty use social media.* Babson Park, MA: Babson Survey Research Group.

Nackerud, S., & Scaletta, K. (2008). Blogging in the academy. *New Directions for Student Services*, no. 124, 71–87.

Newport, C. (2016). Quit social media. Your career may depend on it. *New York Times.* Retrieved from http://www.nytimes.com/2016/11/20/jobs/quit-social-media-your-career-may-depend-on-it.html?_r=0

Ovadia, S. (2014). ResearchGate and Academia.edu: Academic social networks. *Behavioral and Social Sciences Librarian, 33*(3), 165–169.

Pacheco-Vega, R. (2013, September 28). A summary of curators and social media hashtags for academics [Web log post]. Retrieved from http://www.raulpacheco.org/2013/09/a-summary-of-curators-and-social-media-hashtags-for-academics/

Parker, S. (2016). A long list of Instagram statistics that marketers need to know. *Hootsuite.* Retrieved from https://blog.hootsuite.com/instagram-statistics/

Perrin, A. (2015). Social media usage: 2005–2015. *Pew Research Center*. Retrieved from http://www.pewinternet.org/2015/10/08/social-networking-usage-2005-2015/

Powell, D. A., Jacob, C. J., & Chapman, B. J. (2012). Using blogs and new media in academic practice: Potential roles in research, teaching, learning and extension. *Innovative Higher Education, 37*(4), 271–282.

Priem, J., Piwowar, H. A., & Hemminger, B. M. (2012). Altmetrics in the wild: Using social media to explore scholarly impact. *arXiv.org.* Retrieved from https://arxiv.org/abs/1203.4745

Reich, E. S. (2011). Online reputations: Best face forward. *Nature, 473*, 138–139. Retrieved from http://www.nature.com/news/2011/110511/full/473138a.html

Riesch, H., & Mendel, J. (2014). Science blogging: Networks, boundaries and limitations. *Science as Culture, 23*(1), 51–72.

Roblyer, M. D., McDaniel, M., Webb, M., Herman, J., & Witty, V. (2010). Findings on Facebook in higher education: A comparison of college faculty and student uses and perceptions of social networking sites. *The Internet and Higher Education, 13*(3), 134–140.

Ronson, J. (2015). *So you've been publicly shamed.* New York, NY: Riverhead Books.

Ross, C., Terras, M., Warwick, C., & Welsh, A. (2011). Enabled backchannel: Conference Twitter using by digital humanists. *Journal of Documentation, 67*(2), 214–237.

Scalzi, J. (2016). Who we are online, who we are offline, how they're different and how they're the same. *Whatever.* Retrieved from http://whatever.scalzi.com/2016/09/24/who-we-are-online-who-we-are-offline-how-theyre-different-and-how-theyre-the-same/

Seaman, J., & Tinti-Kane, H. (2013). *Social media for teaching and learning.* Boston, MA: Pearson Learning and Babson Survey Research Group. Retrieved from http://www.onlinelearningsurvey.com/reports/social-media-for-teaching-and-learning-2013-report.pdf

Shives, K., & Sanders, A. (2013). Intro to resumes for CV-minded academics. *Inside Higher Ed.* Retrieved from https://www.insidehighered.com/blogs/gradhacker/intro-resumes-cv-minded-academics

Signorelli, J. (2012). *Storybranding.* Austin, TX: Greenleaf Book Group Press.

Smith, A. (2015). U.S. smartphone use in 2015. *Pew Research Center.* Retrieved from http://www.pewinternet.org/2015/04/01/us-smartphone-use-in-2015/

Smith, J. (2013). Why every job seeker should have a personal website, and what it should include. *Forbes.* Retrieved from http://www.forbes.com/sites/jacquelynsmith/2013/04/26/why-every-job-seeker-should-have-a-personal-website-and-what-it-should-include/#6d06ada8902e

Solum, L. B. (2006). Blogging and the transformation of legal scholarship. *Washington University Law Review, 84*, 1071–1088.

Staiger, J. (2003). Authorship approaches. In D. Gerstner & J. Staiger (Eds.), *Authorship and film* (pp. 27–60). New York, NY: Routledge.

Statistics. (2016). *YouTube*. Retrieved from https://www.youtube.com/yt/press/statistics.html

Stats. (2016). *Facebook*. Retrieved from http://newsroom.fb.com/company-info/

Straumsheim, C., Jaschik, S., & Lederman, D. (2015). Faculty attitudes on technology. *Inside Higher Ed*. Retrieved from https://www.insidehighered.com/system/files/media/Faculty%20Attitudes%20on%20Technology%202015.pdf

Taylor, M. (2013). Exploring the boundaries: How altmetrics can expand our vision of scholarly communication and social impact. *Information Standards Quarterly, 25*(2), 27–32.

Thelwall, M., Haustein, S., Larivière, V., & Sugimoto, C. R. (2013). Do altmetrics work? Twitter and ten other social web services. *PLoS ONE, 8*(5), e64841.

Thelwall, M., & Kousha, K. (2014). Academia.edu: Social network or academic network? *Journal of the Association for Information Science and Technology, 65*(4), 721–731.

Turkle, S. (2016). *Reclaiming conversation: The power of talk in the digital age*. New York, NY: Penguin.

Turnage, C. (2017, November 2). U. of Tampa fires professor who called Hurricane Harvey "karma" for Texas. *The Chronicle of Higher Education*. Retrieved from https://www.chronicle.com/blogs/ticker/u-of-tampa-criticizes-professor-who-called-hurricane-harvey-karma-for-texas/119867

Twitter usage. (2016). *Twitter*. Retrieved from https://about.twitter.com/company

Tyson, W. (2010). *Pitch perfect: Communicating with traditional and social media for scholars, researchers, and academic leaders*. Sterling, VA: Stylus.

Vaynerchuk, G. (2013). *Jab, jab, jab, right hook: How to tell your story in a noisy social world*. New York, NY: Harper Business.

Veletsianos, G. (2012). Higher Education Scholars' Participation and Practices on Twitter. *Journal of Computer Assisted Learning, 28*(4), 336–349.

Veletsianos, G. (2016a). *Social media in academia: Networked scholars*. New York, NY: Routledge.

Veletsianos, G. (2016b). Three cases of hashtags used as learning and professional development environments. *TechTrends, 61*(3), 284–292.

Veletsianos, G., & Kimmons, R. (2013). Scholars and faculty members' lived experiences in online social networks. *The Internet and Higher Education, 16*(1), 43–50.

Veletsianos, G., & Shaw, A. (2017). Scholars in an increasingly open and digital world: Imagined audiences and their impact on scholars' online participation. *Learning, Media and Technology, 43*(1), 1–14.

Warner, J. (2016). Why you may need social media for your career. *Inside Higher Ed*. Retrieved from https://www.insidehighered.com/blogs/just-visiting/why-you-may-need-social-media-your-career

Wilentz, S. (2015). Constitutionally, slavery is no national institution. *New York Times*. Retrieved from https://www.nytimes.com/2015/09/16/opinion/constitutionally-slavery-is-no-national-institution.html?_r=0

Yensen, J. (2012). Mentoring and performance support for graduate students using Google+. *Online Journal of Nursing Informatics (OJNI), 16*(3), n.p.

Yu, M., Wu, Y. J., Alhalabi, W., Kao, H., & Wu, W. (2016). ResearchGate: An effective altmetric indicator for active researchers? *Computers in Human Behavior, 55*, 1001–1006.

Zoref, L. (2015). *Mindsharing: The art of crowdsourcing everything*. New York, NY: Penguin.